Backsliding
the bitter bite of beelzebub

The Leaving
Prevention
The Return

by Shirley Buxton

Insignia
PUBLICATIONS
Sacramento, California

Backsliding—the bitter bite of beelzebub
©2011 Shirley Buxton

ISBN 978-0-9823912-5-9
Library of Congress Control Number: 2011937678

Unless otherwise noted, all Scripture quotations in this book are from the King James version of the Bible.

Printed in the United States of America

Published by Insignia Publications
Sacramento, California
(916) 669-1100
www.insigniabooks.com
Cover art and interior layout by Matt Jones

For additional copies contact:
Forrest Press
724 W. 26th St., San Bernardino, CA 92405
(909) 882-6999
shirleybuxton@gmail.com

US $14.99

To Michael, my inspiration

Acknowledgements

Every breath I take is a gift. I acknowledge God and thank Him for the small bit of talent and intellect I possess. I am aware that a slight aberration in my chemical makeup or a slim cerebral accident could cast me in the role of a senseless, incapable woman. I am grateful for God's favor.

Jerry has been an unflagging support as I worked with this book. Throughout our marriage, he has shown himself to be an exceptionally loving husband, and has consistently encouraged my writing projects. Again, Jerry, I thank you for your tolerance of my feisty, adventurous nature, and for the large amount of time I spend writing.

Only you who know her can understand how precious is my only daughter, Rebecca. Subjected to raw breaks in life, she is a rare person, of incredible strength and of brilliant fortitude. She read every word of this manuscript, raising questions of clarity, and noting errors of style, form, and grammar. Thank you, Rebecca.

Another Rebecca, Rebecca Monks is invaluable to me. With painstaking skill, she edited this book, and, patiently (I hope), guided me through the mysterious complexity of the English language.

Thanks to Matt Jones and his staff at Insignia Publications for their skill in designing a beautiful book.

To you who read my work and who ask for more, I give my sincere thanks.

Table of Contents

Introduction

It has been distressing through the years, as I worked in churches, to observe the large number of people who begin a walk with Jesus Christ but who, for one reason or another, fall away and continue no longer with Him. On occasion, this falling away occurs quickly after their new birth, well before they are settled, while at other times, such backsliding occurs after a person has served God many years. In some cases, a cause may be cited—an offense, a deep disappointment, or a misunderstanding. In other instances, no particular moment is noted as the beginning of the regression; rather, a slow drifting is seen.

Within these early paragraphs, I want to emphasize that no part of the book's theme is that of castigating those who have fallen away. Nor have I set myself as arbitrator in determining which of us should be labeled as such. I am not here as a judge or even to serve as a *fruit inspector*. Far beyond the scope of this book, and extending well beyond my intention, is that of identifying backsliders or of analyzing lines to see who may have crossed one. For starters, no one set me up as a judge, and beside that, I wouldn't know how to judge if it were my job. I do not have the skills. Sometimes I even disagree with myself, through the years having been known to change my mind about this or that. It would be difficult for me to judge others, for the most telling of each of us is invisible. That place seen only by God is our heart, our soul, our innermost being.

Now don't misunderstand me here at the beginning. I believe in lines. Lines exist. Lines are good. Every balanced person acknowledges lines. Every church has lines. Every church has standards. God has lines. If we cross over lines God has set, we make dreadful mistakes. Stepping over a line—or not—will determine where we spend eternity. Let it not be thought that my intent is to suggest we should now ignore lines, limits, and standards. Lines are as important now as they ever were—perhaps more so. Pastors and parents need to clearly define them, and we who are of their charge should carefully heed their words.

In contrast to this book being that of a judgmental nature, I hope I have succeeded in presenting my thoughts and concerns in a loving, logical way. Should you note something that would cause a jolt in your spirit, a flash of conviction, or an alert, I trust you will respond in the same tenor with which I have penned the words. As I speak to you, I am clutched by raw conviction; I am overwhelmed by the thought of God's noble ways and of my pitiable state. I weep as I repent. My weary head has known the sting of pain and the ecstasy of truth. I sit beside you. I live on your street.

So no, I will not judge, for in no way am I competent to do so. But all who read this book are in danger. Satan's rancid breath is burning down our backs. His hot stench belches onto our necks; his odious arms stretch to snare us and to pull us down into hell. We need help. We don't want to fall away. We don't want to backslide. As you read here, you will find an abundance of Scripture, for there we find our answers, our map, and the day-by-day directives that will take us from this evil world to one of righteousness. Hear me, please. Learn this. Know that Scripture is of ultimate power, containing such energy as truly cannot be imagined. Within the spirit world, the Word of God is mightily feared. Satan trembles in his pasty skin when he hears the Word. Distinctive lines are marked on the pages of our Bibles. What seem to some but suggestion and proposal is actually mandate and injunction. Scripture doesn't stagger. Its pages do not molder and fall to the ground, torn and degraded. The Word of God is of fire. It is a hammer.

"Is not my word like as a fire? saith the LORD; and like a hammer that breaketh the rock in pieces?" (Jer. 23.29).

So, to you who are in danger of backsliding, which I hope you understand is all of us, I point you to Scripture, to God's Word. Fiery. Strong.

Within every community of any size live backsliders. You may pass them every day, intermeddle with them in the marketplace, at the bank, at the automotive garage, or in the insurance office, never recognizing who they are. At other times, backsliders are easily identifiable. Indeed, they may vocalize such a designation and take one of many stances: defensive, apologetic, ashamed, puzzled, or arrogant.

And so I write. I write of backsliding with the dream that these few pages will snatch back into the fold one who has wandered. I write of backsliding on the chance that its warning will preclude a disillusioned teenager or a broken adult from abandoning a walk with Jesus. I write of backsliding to urge the godly to manifest considerable care in relationships and in ministry. I write of backsliding to extend hope to the wayward, and finally, I write of backsliding to tell the story of my second-born son, Michael, who for more than 25 years trudged the prodigal's rough and rocky course but who because of God's grace and mercy has regained his rightful place as a son of God. His feet are now fixed in an unswerving design on that high and holy way. His story of redemption and its aftermath is staggering. The measure of its faith-building results is inestimable. To every godly parent who through the black night whispers the name of a wandering child, I bring you hope. Let the story of Michael shape a legitimate dream of that child's return.

Forever will I be grateful. Never will I forget.

Section I

The Leaving

When we lived in Orange County, CA one of our church families lived down the street from us, a family who experienced serious spiritual and marital difficulties and who for a while had not attended church. We had done our best to help, had visited and counseled them, but the prospect of reconciliation appeared bleak. One day there was a rap at our door, my husband answered, and there stood one of their children.

"Hello," Jerry said to the little boy who was about five or six years old. He invited the youngster in, and after a brief conversation inquired about his parents.

"Oh, they quit loving Jesus and they backfired!"

The sight of that beautiful child confessing that his parents had *backfired* was amusing, and both Jerry and I had smiles over our faces, I'm sure. But within the structure of that line was a depth of loss and emptiness that may strike across eternity. *Backslidden, away from God, lost*—a sad litany of words and phrases that disquiet the discerning, sincere person.

Chapter One
~ The Dream ~

Although the thrust of this piece of writing is not to serve as an apologetic for the concept of backsliding, because there are many who posit that Christians cannot backslide, that once a person is born again there is no chance of their ever being lost, I will deal briefly with that issue. Scripture is the authority on the subject.

Consider these strong words:

"For it is impossible for those who were once enlightened, and have tasted of the heavenly gift, and were made partakers of the Holy Ghost, And have tasted the good word of God, and the powers of the world to come, If they shall fall away, to renew them again unto repentance; seeing they crucify to themselves the Son of God afresh, and put him to an open shame" (Hebrews 6.4-6).

"And the destruction of the transgressors and of the sinners shall be together, and they that forsake the LORD shall be consumed" (Isa. 1.28).

"Ye adulterers and adulteresses, know ye not that the friendship of the world is enmity with God? whosoever therefore will be a friend of the world is the enemy of God" (Jas. 4.4).

Psalm 51.11-12 records the piercing wail of David after his dreadful escapade with Bathsheba. David, the sweet psalmist, the one identified as a man after God's own heart, acknowledges his horrific sin and pleads for mercy:

"Cast me not away from thy presence; and take not thy holy spirit from me. Restore unto me the joy of thy salvation; and uphold me with thy free spirit."

So then, we are wise to consider that no one is exempt from the threat of backsliding. Well do I recall a startling event that occurred when I was a young minister's wife. A friend of ours—also a minister—found that his wife was involved in an adulterous relationship. The ghastly end was a destroyed home. This couple pastored in the same state as we, and our ages ranged close. We had shared meals, and our children were friends who played together at conferences and camp meetings. It was shocking.

This experience troubled me. I was puzzled, and frankly, for a while I was fearful. My fear arose because of my knowing well this person, her background, and her history. She was from an exceptional, devout family and was a person who gave no indication of spiritual weakness.

I was born into a Pentecostal minister's home, was filled with the Holy Ghost at the age of ten, and although I have never been in a state that at all approaches perfection, I have never backslidden. Nor have I in any way contemplated such a thought. I reckoned with myself those many years ago as I considered my friend's falling: *Can satan do something to me that he has never done before? Is it possible the devil can tempt me so that I too will fall?*

The word of other people's backsliding astonished me. Although I did not know her, once I learned of a minister's wife who had committed suicide. My mind raced: *Will this woman who had been my sister in His work stand before God as a backslider? How could this be?*

When she was a teenager, my beautiful sister, Donna, left the church in a defiant way. For the remainder of her life, though extremely talented, she veritably staggered through life, as lacking in direction as a drunken star cast in midnight sky. With no benefit of connection with God's church, she lived from crisis to crisis, and then she died—alone, a backslider. It is not easy to write so, and God forbid that I stand in judgment of anyone, certainly not of my darling sister. Instead, I soothe myself with the thought of a loving and merciful God, His shed blood, and His abiding grace. But integrity and caution warn me of God's sinless nature and of His intolerance for iniquity.

Michael, our second-born, was a charming, blond, curly-haired child whom we dedicated and gave back to God when he was but a baby, as we did our other three children. My husband was a pastor,

I was a stay-at-home mom, and although Jerry and I do not claim to have been perfect parents, I think it accurate to call us typical middle-class people who loved God and who lived by His precepts. We were an affectionate, stable family.

Exhibiting musical ability at an early age, Michael became an accomplished drummer. He received the Holy Ghost when he was eight years old, I believe. I treasure the picture that shows him in an aqua-colored bathrobe that was too large as his dad baptized him at our church in Garden Grove, CA. He was a sweet, easily disciplined child. We sent him to youth camps and took him to youth conferences, summer camp meetings, and fellowship meetings. We taught him to pray, to read the Bible, to pay tithe from the money he earned at his small jobs, and to be faithful. We spoke of morality, integrity, and of social graces.

Something went wrong, though, and when he became a teenager, he strayed. Finally, he moved away from home and no longer claimed to be a Spirit-filled child of God. He was a backslider. My baby, my sweet child Michael, was now under the influence of satan. It was a cruel, sharp reckoning and one that brought me unspeakable grief.

Throughout the years of Michael's wanderings, Jerry and I maintained a warm relationship with him and with his family, although our goals and worldview now significantly differed, so that our times together were not as easy and free as we would have liked. Backsliding did not change Michael's personality, of course, and he was as thoughtful and courteous as ever. Although he had taken now to smoke and drink, I never glimpsed him with a cigarette, a whiskey glass, or a can of beer. He was too caring and too respectful to have subjected us to that.

For much was I thankful. Michael did not become bitter, nor did he blame the church or blame us. Once he said, "Dad, I don't want you to feel it was your doing anything wrong that caused me to be this way. That is not the case. This is all my fault." God blessed Michael financially. He founded a construction company and became a wealthy man. I was proud of him and told him so.

But my pride at his many abilities and accomplishments was more than counterbalanced by my regard of his failed marriages, troubled children, and soul-emptiness. Always tender, when he went to church with us and an invitation was extended, he would invariably go to the altar. He knelt and sobbed, and from time to time, he made feeble unsuccessful attempts to serve God. He loved the church, loved God's people, and inquired often about certain ones. I daresay he loved God, although his actions at that time certainly did not affirm that.

The Word of God convinces me that heaven is real and that one day God's people will inhabit that glorious place. Logic and honesty stipulate that I also believe in hell, since its existence and description spring from the same holy book as do the rapturous words that speak of heaven.

These conclusions prescribed thoughts of Michael's spending eternity in hell. It was ghastly to consider, and at night when such vision spread its hot grip over my mind, I pled for God's mercy. Finally, I would be able to shut off that specter and God would give me peaceful sleep, for what mother can retain her sanity while thinking of the eternal destruction of her child?

We did not nag at Michael nor berate him; only occasionally did we talk to him about God and about his future. Once, long years into his backslidden state, I was so troubled and so afraid for him that I invited him to lunch for the express purpose of reminding him of his probable destination. "Mike, the chances are that you will spend eternity in hell." To this day, I don't know how I had the courage to say that to him, but though the words were piercing, they were spoken in love, and Michael knew that.

He pushed back his plate, and I will never forget the wild-eyed blanching of his beloved face. Silence. My plate of food also remained untouched, and I cannot even recall the end of the conversation. (We've laughed since about my ridiculous choice of a place to tell a person he's heading for hell. Hard to think of chewing a cheeseburger in the middle of such an exchange.)

Once, when Michael was in a church service with us, I was so burdened that as I knelt at the altar, I began screaming aloud, "God save my son. Please don't let him be lost." Michael came to me, knelt down, wrapped his arms about me, and whispered, "Don't, Mom. Please don't." (I don't generally recommend such public praying, and I can't think of another occasion where I have done so.)

In August of 2004, Jerry and I were in Santa Maria, CA attending the Western District summer camp meeting. In the night, Jerry dreamed that Michael had been killed. The dream was of such vividness that he related it to me.

Andrew is our youngest son, and he and Michael are extremely close, to the extent that they talk nearly every day by telephone, sometimes more than once. Unknown to us, on the same night of Jerry's unsettling dream, Andrew had a similar one. The details differed, but the ending was the same: Michael was killed.

In the morning after he awoke, Andrew called his brother, who was on vacation in Montana, and told him of the dream. In the evening, still troubled, Jerry rang Michael's number and told of his own. Silence. Then Mike spoke: "Dad, do you know about Andrew's dream?"

"No."

"Andrew called this morning and told me the same thing. Last night, he too dreamed I had been killed."

Chapter Two
Comprehending

I n the beginning pages of this book, it is prudent for us to examine the kernel of backsliding, establish a sound definition, and probe its essence, particularly as regards interpretation in God's Word. It is impossible to rationally discuss a subject without an understanding of the meaning of the theme.

The general use of the word *backslide* calls up lapse, regress, weaken, lose one's resolve, give in to temptation, go astray, and leave the *straight and narrow*. *Error* and *fall off the wagon* are other words and terms that speak to the secular use of the word *backsliding*.

The spiritual sense of the word includes most of these but presses more deeply to encompass the vision of these expressions with respect to the human soul. It is one thing to fall off the wagon as regards a low-carbohydrate diet or to regress from one's daily regimen of a three-mile run. It is quite another to backslide in the spiritual sense of the word, for such action circumscribes an awful turning-back from God, from heavenly ambition, and from considerations of the Spirit.

Backsliding speaks to changing course, so that instead of mounting higher on the road to heaven, the backslider is now in a spiraling descent. God is no longer the focus of his life. His ambitions have deteriorated; he disregards God and His Word. A backslider turns from God (I Kings 11.9). He buckles and twists, becoming ever more distorted as he looks the other way. This is the man who was created in the image of God and who was ordained to serve and to worship Him. Once, backsliders faced God's way and walked boldly, secure in their standing as cherished children. Well positioned, they exuded peace and contentment. Now, though, they have recanted; they have gone back on their commitments, on their dedications, on their vows.

To consider that I would ever turn from God appalls me. How could I? What could plunge me to such depth, to such cavernous waste?

I cringe to imagine my back against God, my face fronting satan and his treacherous deceitfulness. I quail at the thought of satan's leer, as his despicable mouth and hot breath would whisper vile thoughts and plans into my head and into my soul. And of Paul's accusation to the Galatians in verse 9 of chapter 4, I distinctly note: "But now, after that ye have known God, or rather are known of God, how turn ye again to the weak and beggarly elements…?" Now that I know the exhilaration of sitting in the very presence of God and of having His strength and force, indeed His sheer being living inside me, (Don't ask me how such is possible, for I cannot answer, except that I know it to be true.) how could I possibly turn to that of weakness, ineffectiveness, and a vile nature?

Be aware that turning from God is not a neutral act, for such action necessitates the serving of a new master. The backslider has discarded God's Word as his marker and instead has chosen criteria from the evil one. When a backslider turns from God, invariably—for he has no other choice—he turns toward satan (1 Tim. 5.15). With confused and clouded eye, he joins the rank of evil, of the iniquitous (Ps. 125.5).

In glorious days now past, the backslider was in love with Jesus Christ, with the church, and with its people. Now he has lost that emotion—that first precious love—and is engaged in a new relationship, an affair that, however gleaming and exciting it may appear, can only lead to loss and to perdition. In the final book of the Bible, the Revelation of Jesus Christ—2nd chapter, John records Jesus' indictment. Directed to the church at Ephesus, the words in the first part of the chapter are complimentary ones as Jesus acknowledges their labor, patience, hatred of evil, and perseverance. But something had happened along the way, and in verse 4, Jesus speaks these pathetic words: "Nevertheless I have somewhat against thee, because thou hast left thy first love."

Oh, shocking and awful words: You have left your first love. You have gone away. You are turned now to a new lover.

God recognized that His beloved people, the Israelites, were a stubborn group, and He did not spare telling the world about it. He went so far as to accuse them of harlotry and referred to them as a "backsliding heifer" (Hos. 4.15-16). Once He called them "backsliding children" and another time a "backsliding daughter" (Jer. 3.22 and 31.22).

How galling to consider that a backslider now is rejecting God's

Word and is turning from the Gospel. Paul speaks to the Galatians of this grim framework in chapter 1, verses 6 and 7, ending with the words, "There be some that trouble you, and would pervert the gospel of Christ." Pervert the Gospel? How could I entangle myself with satan's devices so that I stoop to disdain and deride God's holy Word? How could it be so? Such behavior, unthinkable to one who walks in the Spirit, preposterous to the mind of a man who has not fallen, is inevitable in the culture of the backslidden. The judgment of the backslider has declined: satan has warped his thinking. Paul continues his forceful preaching: You're "bewitched," he says, "O foolish Galatians" (Gal. 3.1).

On no account will the human vessel remain empty, and to fill the painful void the stripping of God's Spirit has generated, the backslider turns toward the world. The world that once he disdained, the world in which he had no interest, the world he avoided, now beckons, its bling a magnet to his gutted soul. To the world he turns, for there is left no other place. Ask Paul. Ask Demas.

"For Demas hath forsaken me, having loved this present world..." (2 Tim 4.10).

You're again entangled in the world, Peter charges, then advances into the terrible warning at the end of verse 20 and into verse 21 of 2 Peter, chapter 2:

"...the latter end is worse with them than the beginning. For it had been better for them not to have known the way of righteousness, than, after they have known it, to turn from the holy commandment delivered unto them."

To do so is to slug about as animals in their waste, Peter scorns:

"But it is happened unto them according to the true proverb, The dog is turned to his own vomit again; and the sow that was washed to her wallowing in the mire" (2 Pet. 2.22).

An interesting observation is that although the concept of backsliding is conclusively found in the New Testament, no form of the word *backslide* is actually seen there. Already we have discussed falling away and backsliding in regard to Demas and both the Galatian and the Ephesian churches. Paul goes on to use such terms as "Purge out the old leaven" (1 Cor. 5.7) and "Fornication is reported among you" (1 Cor. 5.1). Paul implied that Hymaenaeus and Alexander were backsliders, saying that concerning faith, they "have made shipwreck" (1 Tim. 1.19-20). Paul speaks again of those fallen from grace:

"This thou knowest, that all they which are in Asia be turned away from me; of whom are Phygellus and Hermogenes" (2 Tim. 1.15).

Jesus, Himself, says a backslider is not fit:

"...No man, having put his hand to the plough, and looking back, is fit for the kingdom of God" (Luke. 9.62).

Frightening words are written in Mark 3.29:

"But he that shall blaspheme against the Holy Ghost hath never forgiveness, but is in danger of eternal damnation:"

Strongly, I caution you. Chain your tongue and capture your evil thoughts. For who can say where is chalked the line over which one may pass—and never return.

An unbroken theme throughout the Bible, from Genesis to Revelation, is that of backsliding. Genesis, you say? Yes, Genesis, for would it not be on the mark to note Adam and Eve as the first backsliders? Did they not fall from grace? Were they not cast from the presence of God because of sin?

One last thought concerning the definition and essence of backsliding. Backsliding is seldom consummated—probably never—in one fell swoop. It is a condition of degrees. This turning from God, this losing the first love, this falling away—this backsliding—comes gradually, a notch, a rung, a step at a time. A chain of chance is braided: flawed conversation, sinful decisions, a faulty turn, miscalculations, a lingering look. Thus begins the dip.

Chapter Three
God's Emotions Regarding Sin and Backsliding

G od does not take well to backsliding. God is holy and pure. His attributes set Him in opposition to sin and the sinful. We have already noted this when in the book of Hosea He called His own people a heifer. *You are a backsliding heifer, Israel.* Backsliding, regardless of the variant name attached to the form, is always seen in the Bible as a serious condition. People commonly paint God as a sweet pacifist who is long-suffering and who at the end of every person's life says, "Come on up here in heaven and be with me." Not so, my friend. Yes, God is accommodating and loving, but let us not forget His other side, His holy and righteous nature that cannot abide sin. Let us consider these scriptures that point to God's displeasure with sin.

ANGER

"And the LORD was angry with Solomon, because his heart was turned from the LORD God of Israel, which had appeared unto him twice" (1 Kings 11.9).

"And Israel joined himself unto Baalpeor: and the anger of the LORD was kindled against Israel" (Num. 25.3).

"God judgeth the righteous, and God is angry with the wicked every day" (Ps. 7.11).

WRATH-ABHORRENCE

"But turned back, and dealt unfaithfully like their fathers: they were turned aside like a deceitful bow. When God heard this, he was wroth, and greatly abhorred Israel:" (Ps. 78.57-59).

DISPLEASURE

"Nevertheless I have somewhat against thee, because thou hast left thy first love" (Rev. 2.4).

GRIEF

"And it repented the LORD that he had made man on the earth, and it grieved him at his heart" (Gen. 6.6).

Perhaps God had brooded over His world for some time, grieving, as He saw the backsliding and sinfulness of the people He had created. But it is in verse 7 that we hear first hear God speak His plan. He was grieved, yes, but He was also angry. What an amazing story unfolds here as God said, *I'll kill them. I'm sorry that in the beginning I even made those people.*

One man found grace, and because of Noah and his family, the immense ark was raised. For those who were obedient, God provided a way to escape the punishment that was coming. Noah preached, hammered, suffered ridicule, preached, and hammered some more. Finally came the day when the skies darkened, thunder roared, and it began to rain.

"And every living substance was destroyed which was upon the face of the ground, both man, and cattle, and the creeping things, and the fowl of the heaven; and they were destroyed from the earth: and Noah only remained alive, and they that were with him in the ark" (Gen. 7.23).

INDIGNATION

"For, behold, the LORD cometh out of his place to punish the inhabitants of the earth for their iniquity: the earth also shall disclose her blood, and shall no more cover her slain" (Isa. 26.21).

HATE

"These six things doth the LORD hate: yea, seven are an abomination unto him: A proud look, a lying tongue, and hands that shed innocent blood, An heart that deviseth wicked imaginations, feet that be swift in running to mischief, A false witness that speaketh lies, and he that soweth discord among brethren" (Prov. 6.16-19).

VEXATION

"But they rebelled, and vexed his holy Spirit: therefore he was turned to be their enemy, and he fought against them" (Isa. 63.10).

Although I had read this verse many times, well do I recall when I first took particular note of it and when I considered its awful ramifications. Think about it. God was so disgusted with the Israelites, His own, His chosen people, that He fought against them! Read about it in Leviticus 26.25:

"And I will bring a sword upon you, that shall avenge the quarrel of my covenant: and when ye are gathered together within your cities, I will send the pestilence among you; and ye shall be delivered into the hand of the enemy."

And in Jeremiah 21.5-7:

"And I myself will fight against you with an outstretched hand and with a strong arm, even in anger, and in fury, and in great wrath. And I will smite the inhabitants of this city, both man and beast: they shall die of a great pestilence. And afterward, saith the LORD, I will deliver Zedekiah king of Judah, and his servants, and the people, and such as are left in this city from the pestilence, from the sword, and from the famine, into the hand of Nebuchadrezzar king of Babylon, and into the hand of their enemies, and into the hand of those that seek their life: and he shall smite them with the edge of the sword; he shall not spare them, neither have pity, nor have mercy."

Those are terrifying Scriptures, Scriptures that chill me as I consider how strongly God feels about backsliding and how angry He becomes with those who stubbornly turn from Him. And so with David, as I consider my evil ways, I repent. Sincerely, do I plead for God's mercy, for it is dreadful to think of being on the wrong side of battle—to think of God fighting against me.

On an earlier page, I spoke contrary to those who would have us see God as all loving, and as being tolerant of sin, so that every man at his death is admitted to heaven. On the past page or two, I have addressed the issue of God's strong and fearful emotions and actions. Without negating my previous thought that God is holy and that sin cannot stand before Him, I want to close this chapter by listing some of His loving and kind attributes. With gratitude and assurance, we think of these, for without this pivotal understanding, there could be no meaningful discussion of backsliding. We would be without dream, bereft, and lost, for all of us have sinned, all have come short, all stand in need of God's mercy.

LOVE

"For God so loved the world, that he gave his only begotten Son, that whosoever believeth in him should not perish, but have everlasting life" (John 3.16).

This is the theme of the Bible: God's love for man.

REPENTANCE

"O house of Israel, cannot I do with you as this potter? saith the LORD. Behold, as the clay is in the potter's hand, so are ye in mine hand, O house of Israel. At what instant I shall speak concerning a nation, and concerning a kingdom, to pluck up, and to pull down, and to destroy it; If that nation, against whom I have pronounced, turn from their evil, I will repent of the evil that I thought to do unto them" (Jer. 18.6-8).

PATIENT

"The LORD is gracious, and full of compassion; slow to anger, and of great mercy" (Ps. 145.8).

LONGSUFFERING

"And shall not God avenge his own elect, which cry day and night unto him, though he bear long with them?" (Luke 18.7).
"The Lord is not slack concerning his promise, as some men count slackness; but is longsuffering to us-ward, not willing that any should perish, but that all should come to repentance" (2 Pet. 3.9).

Joyful

"These things have I spoken unto you, that my joy might remain in you, and that your joy might be full" (John 15.11).

"And now come I to thee; and these things I speak in the world, that they might have my joy fulfilled in themselves" (John 17.13).

Compassion

"In a little wrath I hid my face from thee for a moment; but with everlasting kindness will I have mercy on thee, saith the LORD thy Redeemer" (Isa. 54.8).

I love this verse of Scripture. Indeed the entire 54th chapter is glorious. Think about God's words here. I was angry with you, wrathful to the degree that I couldn't bear to see you. I *punished you by hiding, but with everlasting kindness will **I have mercy** on you!"* Isn't that the greatest scripture—one full of promise and hope. I don't want God's face hid, for I cannot bear the thought of His looking away from me.

In concluding this chapter, let me emphasize again how much God hates sin and how He looks with disdain on backsliding, so much so that He actually turned His back on His chosen people when they wallowed in their sin. He fought against them and hid His face. Surely then, by logical extension and by sanction of Scripture, we must say God sees our backsliding in similar grim fashion—fighting against us, His face turned away, ready to spew us out. But oh, His mercy! At the slightest turn toward God, at the slightest sign of repentance, God reaches down with His unfathomable love, gathers us up, and restores us to our rightful place in Him.

SECTION II
PREVENTION

It was Christmas Eve. Carols played over the Newark Beth Israel Medical Center intercom. Glittering trees festooned the lobby. Throughout the great building, the twinkling of tiny lights mingled with the scent of pine and of holiday. Trimming the patient room walls were gaily-decorated cards, while in the kitchens, the holiday meal neared completion. The atmosphere was thick with the Christmas spirit. In a few hours, it would be Christmas Day.

Cruising the halls of the famed hospital was 22-year-old Martina Allen. Her intentions were evil: She was out to steal a baby. She found one, wrapped her in a blanket, clipped off the security ankle bracelet, and sprinted out the front door.

–As related by Rev. Carlton Coon
May/June 2008 *Director's Communique*

At the Federal Medical Center in Lokoja, Nigeria, on a Tuesday morning around 7:30, Mrs. Fatima Musa lay sleeping, her two-day-old baby ensconced in a snug infant bed beside her. Posing as a relative, a thief entered the room and snatched the child. Jolted awake, the mother looked into the crib and saw that her tiny girl was gone. (nm.onlinenigeria.com)

Ever had a baby disappear from your church? Ever had a newborn snatched from your altars? Director of the Home Missions Division of the United Pentecostal Church, International, Rev. Carlton L. Coon, Sr., raises this provocative question in the May/June 2008 issue of his *Director's Communique*. I am using his discussion as a springboard for this chapter on how compassionate, considerate leadership can help alleviate backsliding.

Closely aligned to this section is the next in which we discuss ways all of us, individually, can protect ourselves from falling away, from the dread of backsliding. At the foundation of these discussions, and interspersed throughout, will be both the cause and the avoidance of backsliding. In this section, the focus will be on the persons who surround, attend, and minister to those who stand a chance of backsliding, which in the broadest sense, is anyone who is a child of God. For once a spiritual birth has taken place, backsliding is possible. Indeed, as miserable as it is to acknowledge, there is great likelihood that a falling away—a slipping back into the world—will occur.

While the substance of this book, as it is a spiritual issue, may seem to be directed toward the church proper, it should be understood that deep concerns around backsliding must reside within the home of every Christian. As parents and other family members, we need to be aware of satan's devices and alive to his trickery and crafty art that may be targeted toward our children. Thus, it must be understood that every caution put forward concerning church activities and methods may apply also in the home. Indeed, there is no more crucial place in which to guard against backsliding than in the home, for of homes and families is the church formed.

As has been mentioned, it rests with the Christian himself to be the first-line of offense against evil. Ultimately, I am accountable for my decisions, my advancement or regression, my growth or withering, my discernment or ignorance, my backsliding into devilry, or my flourishing as a child of God. I reckon with the fact that when I stand before God, I will be the one who will answer for what I have done with my life. I cannot blame my husband, my pastor, my church family, my childhood deprivation, or my family curses. I tremble at the thought, for at the end, I alone will have decided my final destination.

Having said that, however, it cannot be disputed that a significant amount of human nurturing comes from others. Family, friends, the church, and the pastor certainly share some responsibility for the success or failure of every person for whom some oversight is dictated.

This section will look into that fraction of the backsliding issue, certainly with no intent of faultfinding or fixing blame, but rather as part of an honest search for those tools that will effect the saving of every soul possible. From time to time, the thought beats through my mind: Is it believable that someone will be eternally lost because I did not effectively teach, pray, inquire, solicit, or generally care? Did I feel a nudge in my spirit to lift a phone to my ear, to schedule a lunch, to lay a hand on a bent shoulder—and ignore all? Not a pleasant idea, nor one on which to linger, only to honestly consider so that such lapses will not likely occur in my life.

"Ever lose a baby?" Carlton Coon asks, and if he stares our way long enough demanding an answer, I fear we must say, "Yes." We have misplaced babies. We have no idea where they are, and a sad acknowledgement of truth is that sometimes they were long missing before we effectively noted their absence. They were conceived, nourished enough to be born, and survived the birthing room, but now, where are they? Where are the babies? Were they left to tend themselves, to gather their own food, to learn to walk alone with no one to steady them or to lift them?

"Carlton Coon?" you say. He is the one asking of the babies and well he should as a home missions director. But Carlton Coon? How about God? Is that God gazing at me? Is that God popping a quiz concerning my family, my friends, and those new babies down at the church? I shrink at the thought and tremble when I consider staring into the eyes of God while trying to churn out an answer. What does God think of losing babies? What insights are available that will help us forestall backsliding in those for whom we have some responsibility?

Chapter Four
Love People

If I had only one piece of advice to give a young pastor's wife, it would be this: love people, and let them know you do. **This counsel is fitting in every venue, and its positive results will likely be evident** in any situation. People will tolerate our ignorance, lack of experience, lack of talent, and generally most of our mistakes if they know we are sincere and that we care about those to whom we minister—that we love them. Our brothers and sisters in the church are less likely to slip away if they believe they are truly loved, if they understand they will be acutely missed if they should stray.

Parents, your children will be less inclined to resent your words of strong biblical teaching and restrictions if they are sure of your love, if you show affection for them, if you listen as they speak, if you tend their needs. If you nourish them in every way, they are more apt to respond to those times when you must discipline them, when your soul urges you to reel them in from dangerous waters, when you insist they turn from a path that you perceive as treacherous.

We spend time with those we love. Our children need us not only as providers of food and shelter, but also as participants in recreation and in light moments of fun and adventure. Family vacations are important, as during these relaxing days, opportunities often arise in which moral issues may be discussed in an atmosphere where, without the bustle and time constraints of our busy lives, our children may be able to really talk to us, to hear us, to listen. There's nothing quite like a father or a mother sitting creekside with a son or daughter, luxuriating in this incredible world God created for us. Such slow, languid days often lead to conversations that open the clamshell of a child, as it were, revealing inside a fine jewel, a rare and glowing treasure.

Chapter Five
Make Disciples

1: DISCIPLESHIP CLASSES

As crucial to spiritual babies as to physical ones is that of training and instruction. From the simple home to the most prestigious is the sure understanding that a newborn baby cannot walk, nor even sit up or crawl. He has no concept of moral values or of courtesy. When he's hungry, he screws up his face and yelps. When he's tired and through with crying, he lays down his head wherever he is and sleeps. He disregards fashion, modesty, and consideration for others. He's in line for training.

Many who come into our churches are clueless regarding even a generally moral life, much less that of holy living. The Bible is completely unfamiliar, except for its title, so they are as liable to look in the front of their stiff new book for 1 Corinthians as they are in the middle for the one called Exodus. Likely they have never seen a caring, happy marriage lived out, much less had effective parenting modeled for them. Biblical principles and doctrines are as foreign to them as Yiddish is to most of us. They must be taught. If there is any chance of them obeying God's Word and inculcating His principles into their lives, we must teach them, and we must do it quickly, for the challenges they will face in their new lives are formidable.

Providing discipleship training for every new convert is critical. As you take into consideration your facilities, your schedule, and your abilities, you will find a way to effectively teach those babies who are born to you. While it is beyond the scope of this book to make specific recommendations, there are many excellent programs, guidelines, and study aids available.

One more thought on making disciples of new converts is the critical step of assigning one person to stay connected with the new baby. It may be the pastor or the pastor's wife, a small group leader, a grandmother, or the youth leader. Whoever it is, there *must be* someone. Someone who will call, listen, send a note, bake a plate of cookies, sit at the hospital during traumatic days, take a midnight ring …

2: Teaching In Our Homes

Our home lay long in evening quiet last night. My husband was asleep as I tossed on our bed, wakeful, thinking of this portion of the book recalling that I had finished it and had moved into the next section. Something niggled at me, though, something about our homes, children, young people, parents, and about learning. Thus, I speak of my concerns.

Pi is the 16th letter of the Greek alphabet, and it is this small word that is used to indicate a mathematical value of 3 1/7. That's what I recall learning in elementary school, but when I checked this morning, I found the exact mathematical designation of pi to be 3.14159, and that is not even exact, for computation can carry out the digits to thousands more. In school, our children are taught these central facts. They learn the table of chemical elements and their atomic numbers, the rotation pattern of the earth and the names of the planets, and that matter can neither be created nor destroyed. They analyze the structure of language and are taught to spell thousands of words. They learn of history and literature and art. The learning of these basics is decisive, for the well-read person will have knowledge of key facts and a fundamental understanding of the world and how it functions. Ultimate knowledge, however, extends past this point.

Most children in apostolic homes come to comprehend their need of salvation early, and it is not uncommon to see youngsters weeping as the Holy Ghost touches them. Often these are little more than toddlers. I have seen this happen on innumerable occasions throughout my lifetime, and certainly I know of my own early encounters with God. Undeniably, these first spiritual experiences are authentic and enduring.

I'm convinced, however, that there may be little actual understanding of these experiences. If we are to help our children maintain close relationships with God, as maturity allows, we must see that they have full comprehension of Bible salvation. This understanding is as crucial for them as it is for any other new convert, yet typically we don't place them in discipleship classes. Where, then, will they assimilate these truths? The Sunday school class is one place we have relied on for years, and it is plausible to think our youngsters have learned more about the Bible in these settings than in any other place. Across the world, Sunday school teachers have given multiplied thousands of hours to study, to classroom preparation, and to actual Sunday morning teaching of our children. Christian schools have contributed, as have Bible quizzing workers and youth leaders. My own children distinctly benefited from the devotion and sacrifices made by Sunday school and Christian school teachers, and I am quite sure much credit for their godly living today derives from these wonderful people.

I fear, though, that the most obvious place for such teaching has, in the main, been overlooked, and the one with the greatest chance of lasting influence is underutilized. I speak of our homes. Think about it. The most important issue our children will ever face is that of their salvation. They must prepare for life after death, fully understanding that it is by their adherence or non-adherence to Scripture that their eternal destination will be decided. Will it be heaven or will it be hell? These are not words hastily gathered to fill up a page, but within these few lines is a vital question, and one you as a parent cannot avoid. No one other than the child himself is as responsible as you are should he turn away and trudge down the low road of the prodigal. You must decide the weight you give the subject. Your decision is telling.

God pointed to this and speaking of Scripture and the precepts of holy living in Deuteronomy 11.19 says,

> "Teach them to your children, talking about them when you sit at home and when you walk along the road, when you lie down and when you get up" (*New International Version*).

Children and young people are masters at detecting insincerity and phoniness. Little wonder they stray if they see us speak in one mode yet act in another. They may say nothing, but with keen eyes are they looking, and with rapt ears are they listening. If in our homes the guidelines of the church we attend are scoffed at or just ignored, if the clear biblical teaching of separation from the world is a non-issue in our family, in the developing minds and consciences of our children, similar thought pattern and judgment are likely being plotted. If we indulge them and make excuses for their misbehavior, we do them no favor, rather great harm.

Reiterating, I say that Christian homes should be the first bastion of biblical training, with talk of God, the Bible, prayer, worship, and evangelism being a style of living. I've been stunned to see children from apostolic homes routinely fail to say a little prayer of gratitude before their meals. Not long ago, I asked a small boy who has been reared in the church, "What is Easter? Why do we celebrate Easter?"

He tucked his head, stammered a bit, embarrassed, I think. "Uh, is it when Jesus was born? Is that it?" He paused and then finished, "I'm not sure."

Before we proceed, I want to urge you, Christian father, to be a strong spiritual leader, remembering that you are the head of your home. Your wife is not. You are. Look around. Step back. Sincerely consider your family. Think deeply of this deplorable world. Guard your home. Open your eyes. Judge the dress of your daughters before they go out the front door. Analyze the screens that sit about your home. It would be a grim oversight were I not to mention the perils that may be introduced into our homes by way of television sets, computers, the Internet, smart phones, and video games. Be wise. Be authentic. Be consistent. Recall that this book is about backsliding and its prevention. I'm strongly suggesting that a crucial way to help fend off this turning away from God is that fathers insure godly standards in their homes.

In no way would I suggest that Christian mothers are less important in seeing that righteousness prevails in the home than are fathers. It simply is not a matter of one being more significant than the other; rather, by modeling godly living and by establishing a righteous atmosphere in their home, a couple is working together toward the common goal of saving their children. Actually, far too often, a mother may be forced to take on the leadership role in their home. Either because of his reluctance or because of his absence, the father abdicates such position.

I submit that as thrilling as it is to see our children walk across a stage with cords of honor about their necks, as sensational as it is to see their science fair entries blazing in blue, as pleased as we are to see them diligently work geometry problems around the kitchen table in the evenings, so much more should we be elated as they take up a Bible and in a masterful style, talk of God's ways and of His plan for salvation. We as parents are key to this success, for no one cares as we do. No one else has such opportunity.

A positive comprehension of Scripture including a distinct knowing of biblical requirements is the finest piece of parchment you can place within the warm hand of your child. Not likely is he to stray if these precepts are lodged in his mind, for adherence to the injunction in 1 Peter 3.15 he will easily manifest:

> "But sanctify the Lord God in your hearts: and be ready always to give an answer to every man that asketh you a reason of the hope that is in you with meekness and fear:"

Chapter Six
Sound Teaching and Preaching

I know I'm wading into deep water here (so I'll not stay long), but if as spiritual leaders, either in our homes or in the church, we want our people to have the confidence to follow us, it is pivotal that Scripture backs our teachings. For only God's Word is infallible. Within all other writings, we may suspect error, and though well-intentioned authors may be involved, it is only the Bible that is the breathed voice of God, that is flawless.

At times, of course, ministers may stipulate behavior and dress where an exact description is not found in the Bible but where the principle for such is clear. A pastor may have personal preferences, such as requiring leaders on the platform to wear dress clothes and to be well groomed. Perhaps such men are asked to wear suits and ties, and women are asked to refrain from wearing denim skirts and tennis shoes while participating in Sunday morning worship activities. Clarity, and the development of an atmosphere of integrity, call for the understanding that these measures are not particularly mandated in Scripture, but that they fall under the discretion of the leadership of this particular church. His thinking is that such dress and behavior will enhance the growth and development of this church group.

Has the thought ever occurred to you that you weren't being consistent? Perhaps you have been inconsistent regarding house rules and the discipline of your children. Perhaps you have avoided one activity you consider sinful while at the same time embracing another almost identical one. I confess to have noted inconsistencies in my own life, and because I want to be honest, I have spent time in considering the principles and precepts by which I live. Let us in leadership strive to be reliable, assuring that our teaching is honorable and absolutely aligned with the Word of God.

Without having expressly stated so, I hope I have conveyed the thought that as leaders, we must use extreme care when we speak to others in our churches, either over the pulpit or in an individual setting. Speaking of flaws and misbehaviors of other ministers is especially unwise, for to do so may well shake a believer's confidence in ministry in general. Only today, I learned of a newly-born believer whose pastor—thoughtlessly, I believe, and with no intent to harm— had told him of a negative action another pastor had taken. The new convert was troubled and turned to another person in the church, who it seems has helped smooth over the situation.

Here, I want to remind you who stand behind the pulpit of the power of preaching. I was born into the home of a preacher, married one, and have sons, a grandson, and other family members who are preachers. Among my circle of friends are many preachers. Believe me when I say I've seen them in every stage of life. I've seen them in ragged shirts, with uncombed hair, and at other low and challenging moments. I have been with them when they were fearful, hungry, and needed a nap. I've seen their humanity. Often.

But I've seen these same ones—each of them—step into the pulpit and be changed into an oracle of God. It still astonishes me. After all these years, I tell you, it astonishes me. When I see a mere man transformed by God's anointing into His voice, I tremble—and I listen.

So to my friends, family, and all others who are preachers of the Gospel, I remind you of your great calling, of your tremendous responsibility, and of your divine appointment. In all humility and with meek respect, I urge you to stay our feet from backsliding. I assure you I am weeping as I write these words.

Chapter Seven
~ Superb Church Services ~

In 2007, when I was nearing 70 years old, and when Jerry had already passed that mark, we moved to Lake Havasu City, AZ to pioneer a church. As can be imagined, it was a challenge, especially the church services themselves, for in the beginning, there were only three or four of us. Our little building was pretty quiet, and even as the congregation grew, our new converts did not easily take to our apostolic way of worship. It was foreign to them, and it was a while before they began to pray aloud, to clap their hands, and to raise their arms in praise to God.

Among the founding bunch, I was the one who played the tiny keyboard that was hooked up to a fine little amplifier and that was later routed through the portable sound system our son Mike bought at a pawnshop. After a time, we were given a better keyboard; then came the day when Rev. Jerry Rowell gave us a Hammond C3. It was marvelous. Now we could really have church! Mike is an accomplished drummer, and early on, he arranged his set in the church, although the problem was he was also the song leader. Most of the time, the drums were silent. Sometimes though, as the church developed and when we sang a lively song, Mike would leave the pulpit and head over to his drums. I knew this was a signal that I was now the song leader, and that I was to sing into my microphone. These were exhilarating, productive moments, and in the congregation, the people grinned and learned to worship.

In the first days, when the services seemed a bit stilted and were sometimes awkward, I recall having the distinct resolve to wholly invest myself in each service—singing, playing, and worshipping as though there were hundreds there instead of a dozen or so. It wasn't always easy, for at times, when I looked from my place, I saw only staring, unmoved faces. Sometimes, I just closed my eyes.

My point in telling you this is to emphasize that having vibrant church services is a tremendous deterrent to backsliding. The services should be sincerely prayed over, attention given to the selection of the songs that will be sung, and careful thought concerning the order of the service, always with the consideration that the focal point of each service is the preaching of the Word of God. A dynamic, friendly attitude should pervade the sanctuary, whether it is a magnificent, newly built edifice or a humble storefront. A comfortable, compelling feeling should surround each person who enters the church. Peace should pervade the air. It is to be a sanctuary.

"Throw down that cigarette." It was many years ago when we pastored in Garden Grove, CA that Harold Godair laughed and told Jerry about the conversation. Harold was the husband of Lois Godair, who had long been a faithful saint in our church, and he had attended church that Sunday morning. Afterward, when on the church lawn he lit up, Michael, who was five or six years old, walked right up to him and demanded he rid himself of the cigarette. Fortunately, Harold had a great attitude and took no offense at Mike's thoughtless remark, understanding he was but a child.

The concepts in the conversation I had with Michael that long-ago Sunday afternoon are no doubt fitting to mention here as we consider the importance of people having good church experiences. I can say it in a very few words: The discipline and correction of either church members or visitors should be left to the pastor or to others he appoints. That's it. Period.

Having good church services, though, extends beyond that of joyfulness, uplifting worship, and a feeling of welcome. As mentioned before, it should end with a message that speaks distinctly and forcefully to the congregation, and at times, such messages may point with love to the fact that we are sinners and that we need God. Messages should come that preach to us who are already Christians, messages that challenge us to higher levels of godliness and that warn of our devious ways. That is God's plan. Preaching is His decision. Surely that is included in having good church, for it is anointed Bible preaching that will go far toward the suppression of backsliding.

Chapter Eight
~ Quality Social Activities ~

Humans are social beings. Innate in nearly all of us is the desire to be close to others, to socialize, to sit shoulder-to-shoulder for meals, to laugh and cry in tandem, to play together, and to work side by side for a cause. Gangs are thought to attract so many young people for this very reason. Today's youth has been born into a world of shattered social structure. As do we all, they seek family and community camaraderie, and because it is lacking in their homes, they roam about until they find someone who will take them in. They join a gang. They find a family.

Let us think about this as regards social activities in our churches and in our homes. The teaching of separation from the world is firmly positioned in Scripture and is perhaps more germane to us today than at any time in history, given that we live in the midst of a most shocking and vile society. If we have any hope of living godly, righteous lives, we must separate ourselves from the filth and debauchery around us. Don't misunderstand me. I'm not speaking of commune situations, attitudes of superiority, or wrapping ourselves in saintly robes while looking down our noses at the beggar in the gutter, the client at the gaming table, or the woman with numerous visitors throughout the night. No, not at all. For if we are to emulate Jesus, we will go after these very ones, striving to bring them to salvation, attempting to find a way to tell them the good news of the Gospel.

Yet, the doctrine of separation is crucial, viable, and must be taught. Short-sighted of us as leaders, though, it would be to call for this dedication without setting up alternative means to satisfy the human need for socializing. This need is front and center for young people, and if we are to keep them safe within the bounds of the church and if we are to help them avoid backsliding, we must provide recreation and other activities for them. Of tremendous value are youth camps, family camps, rallies, and conferences. Often at these gatherings, lifelong friendships are cemented, and even spouses may be found.

Those may be expensive functions, but cheaper, more easily accomplished ones will work as well: dinners at the church, concerts, parties on the parking lot, church campouts, fishing expeditions, banquets, fundraising activities. The list of acceptable functions is long and will vary from place to place, although principle and expected outcome are the same. To help prevent backsliding, at the very point where we call for separation from the world, we must provide alternate activities for those persons who have chosen to walk along this brilliant way of holiness, who truly desire to keep themselves pure and unsullied.

Chapter Nine
⚬⚬ A Sense of Belonging ⚬⚬

I don't know if they are still hanging there, but I recall walking into the lobby of South Bay Pentecostal Church in Chula Vista, CA, where Art Hodges is the pastor, and seeing large professionally mounted pictures of various people in the church. As I recall, these were pictures not only of the church leaders, but also of diverse people who made up the church body there. I was impressed by this display of honor and of respect. To one degree or another, most of us like to be recognized and appreciated, and we will more likely stay connected with a group in which those attitudes are prevalent. Surely, a sense of belonging will aid in the inhibiting of backsliding.

Though diverse, every person has a talent. Something comes a little easier to each of us than to others—a skill, an inclination, a gift. When appropriate, a place should be made within the church body for the use of that talent, for when we are able to flourish, we develop a stance of fulfillment and of happiness. Not only are we favored, but the church is also. Our art, singing, writing, woodworking, teaching, gardening, speaking, and myriad other skills and talents elevate the church itself and bring glory to God.

When I was a child, my dad was the pastor of a small church in Springfield, MO, a church that actually was considered medium-sized in those days, having an attendance of around 40 to 50 people, as I recall. The church in St. Louis, where Harry Branding was the pastor, was a large, thriving church and was well known among apostolic people in that area and probably even around the country. I was so impressed with the church that I still recall the address as being 13th and Gravois. We attended both special meetings there and regular services, for if a Sunday was included when we visited our relatives in St. Louis, we went to Brother Branding's church.

I remember one visit in particular. I was about 10 years old, and I was likely gawking about the place as we seated ourselves. What happened next was so unexpected and so remarkable that it is chiseled deeply in my mind, even though the remainder of the service, indeed the rest of the day, is relegated to a blank spot in my head. Winfred Black was the assistant pastor of that great church, and somehow he knew I played the violin. Well, to say I played the violin is a stretch, but I did own one, and I did draw the bow over the strings in the public school orchestra.

That exceptional person, the late Brother Winfred Black, left his seat, went somewhere behind the platform, and returned with a violin which he placed on a vacant chair among the musicians. Soon an usher tapped my shoulder and whispered in my ear that Brother Black wanted me to play the violin. I was astonished then and am now at the thoughtfulness of that man, a man who clearly understood the significance of making a person feel noticed and of being needed in the work of God.

Chapter Ten
⚞ *Avoid Giving Offense* ⚟

"Offenses will come," the young person said to me. With a jaunty attitude, he defended his careless actions, citing Scripture: "Offenses will come." At that time, I was in no position to protest his actions or his words, but this afternoon, years later, the words reverberate in my memory. For assuredly follow Jesus' other words: "…but woe unto him through which they come."

Even though I have alluded to this subject previously, it is of such import in our discussion of the role sterling leadership plays in preventing the falling away of people that it needs elaboration. Jesus spoke strongly to the subject, and in chapter 17 of Luke, verses 1 and 2, Jesus issues this vehement warning:

> "…It is impossible but that offences will come: but woe unto him, through whom they come! It were better for him that a millstone were hanged about his neck, and he cast into the sea, than that he should offend one of these little ones."

Jesus' own words make it clear that it is no light matter to speak disrespectfully to God's people or to deal harshly with them. No one should construe that I am speaking against forceful and direct teaching or that I am suggesting caution and restraint to an extent that failure to preach the whole Word of God would be the result. Nor should I be thought as calling for the disregard of sin. No. There definitely is a time and a place for a *thou art the man* accusation and for the subsequent discipline, which, admittedly, may at times seem harsh.

"Attitudes Make The Man." I heard someone preach a sermon with that title many years ago, so many that the name of the minister is long beyond recollection. The essence of the sermon, though, is etched in my mind and in my soul. Could it be as we deal with our friends, church family, and blood family that our attitudes—whether positive or negative—may be reckoned a major factor in the outcome of any situation? God help me to deal in tenderness with those around me. Stay me from causing offense, certainly from such hurt as might lead to any Christian's backsliding.

Jacob knew of compassion and kindness, and come morning after that night of his life-changing encounter with God, he spoke to his brother, Esau:

> "But Jacob said to him, 'My lord knows that the children are tender and that I must care for the ewes and cows that are nursing their young. If they are driven hard just one day, all the animals will die. So let my lord go on ahead of his servant, while I move along slowly at the pace of the droves before me and that of the children, until I come to my lord in Seir'" (*NIV*, Gen. 33.13-14).

In the first verse of the 15th chapter, Paul addresses the Romans, laying out advice that is as timely today as it was for those New Testament Christians: "We then that are strong ought to bear the infirmities of the weak, and not to please ourselves." When we're dealing with persons who are in a spiritual struggle, and we are stronger, we are to bear with them, to be patient and caring, endeavor to strengthen them, to tend them, to spend time with them, to restore them. It may be inconvenient or even unpleasant, but we do not belong to ourselves anyway, and without God's mercy, none of us would have any hope of being saved.

> "What? Know ye not that your body is the temple of the Holy Ghost which is in you, which ye have of God, and ye are not your own? For ye are bought with a price: therefore glorify God in your body, and in your spirit, which are God's" (1 Cor. 6.19-20).

Recently I learned of a dreadful experience of a young family who do not go to church and who do not claim to be Christians. They were on a short vacation in Las Vegas just before Easter time, and as they were walking around in the city, they observed an outdoor biblical drama. As they paused to watch the action, workers from the church that was producing the drama converged on them, telling them how much they needed God and that if they didn't become Christians, they were going to hell. Not wanting to be part of an ugly scene, the young mom and dad moved on down the sidewalk, but the workers kept following them, shouting loudly that they were going to hell.

Neither the behavior I have related here nor that told in the next few paragraphs are likely to lead anyone to Jesus. More likely an offense will be caused, and a turning away from the Gospel.

A few days ago, a dear minister told me of his son who had fallen away from God and who had been out of the church for some time. One night, being drawn by the Holy Ghost, the son went to church, where at the altar he repented, and regained his place as a child of God. Within a few days, wanting to provide every opportunity for spiritual growth, the father and mother went with their son to a conference in a nearby area. It was a dreadful mistake, for in the middle of the sermon, the evangelist turned to the pastor of the host church and said, "You knew I would do this, didn't you?" He then launched into an ugly litany, where with no visible compassion or loving expression, he harshly named almost every sin imaginable and in a controversial way included activities that few people would consider sinful.

As they drove home that dark night, the son leaned up to the front seat where sat his righteous but grieved mother and father. "I can't take that, Dad," he said. "That's just the reason I can't attend your church." It is my understanding that the young man has never again attended any regular church services.

Even though the father spoke of his disagreement with parts of the message, and certainly with the method of presentation, and though the son knew his father did not agree with such behavior, satan used this sad happening to again hinder this man from serving God. Yes, the young man is responsible for his own action, and yes, he should have the strength to rise above such thoughtless speaking, but he did not, and today, as far as I know, he is lost. He is a backslider.

IT's ME, O LORD

Not my brother, nor my sister, but it's me, O Lord,
Standin' in the need of prayer;
Not my brother, nor my sister, but it's me, O Lord,
Standin' in the need of prayer.

Refrain:
It's me, it's me, O Lord,
Standin' in the need of prayer;
It's me, it's me, O Lord,
Standin' in the need of prayer.

Not the preacher, nor the deacon, but it's me, O Lord,
Standin' in the need of prayer;
Not the preacher, nor the deacon, but it's me, O Lord,
Standin' in the need of prayer.

Not my father, nor my mother, but it's me, O Lord,
Standin' in the need of prayer;
Not my father, nor my mother, but it's me, O Lord,
Standin' in the need of prayer.

Not the stranger, nor my neighbor, but it's me, O Lord,
Standin' in the need of prayer;
Not the stranger, nor my neighbor, but it's me, O Lord,
Standin' in the need of prayer.

—*Negro Spiritual (Public domain)*

AVOID BACKSLIDING BY PERSONAL ACTION

Although personal responsibility has been briefly mentioned as far as the prevention of backsliding is concerned, up to now, the thrust of this book has been to church leaders and to parents, rather than to individuals themselves. Without question, such consideration is timely, even crucial, as we examine backsliding, falling away, or walking no more with God. However we phrase it, the conclusion is the same. We have a person here who once knew God, who, at another time, served Him, but who now has allegiance to a different master, who walks in a contrary direction, and who regards a changed set of values. His list of friends, neighborhood haunts, and worship habits have seen a drastic revision. His worldview has dramatically altered.

Perhaps somewhere in the flux of this great world there exists a person who previously knew God but who backslid and who is proud of the change in his life. Maybe there is one. Maybe there are two. I doubt there are many. I believe the vast majority of persons who once served God and who now serve satan understand their precarious situation, and although they linger before making their way back, they gaze with yearning eye toward those glorious days of fellowship with God. They ache for it.

Blaming others for our shortcomings is convenient, for when we indulge in such behavior, we avoid the painful moment of staring rigidly into our elusive self, the self that is eager to point to others and that is reluctant to point inward. Often with agony are we brought before God who is so gracious as to speak conviction into our spirits. Stammering, we stumble over the foolish words that come from our mouths as we cast about in an effort to fix blame. Urgently, we make great effort to help God see that the fault lies somewhere else, that another person is responsible. But our words are empty and blow about as dried leaves in a dusty place.

Wise am I to press inward and to deal with the certainty that I am responsible for myself. Not another. In my stead will no call to judgment be sounded, nor will one who loves me be sanctioned to mount a defensive shield. No hiding behind the skirt of our mothers or in the wide arms of our fathers. The godliness of no aged saint will speak from our mouths, nor will the strength of that rare and capable young person be a line for our accounting on that dreadful day. No. None else. I will be the one who stands before God. I alone will be positioned for that final examination. Why then do I linger? Why stutter my feet along this perfect way? How is it my eyes lean toward thickness as regards my own faults?

How easy to see flaws in others. How comfortable to gaze on the wrong doing of those about me, even to showcase their imperfections, for when I am in this self-righteous mode, there seems no need to hone my self-probing skills. Certainly, I am not moved toward applying cure to my flawed eye. Picking at the blemishes of others is much more pleasant. Finding fault with our brother rather than with ourselves is not new. In New Testament days, Paul addressed the Christians in Rome:

"But why dost thou judge thy brother? or why dost thou set at nought thy brother? for we shall all stand before the judgment seat of Christ" (Rom. 14.10).

Scripture warns of the approaching day when we will stand before Jesus Christ, and He will judge us. Paul addressed these words to the church at Corinth, but they befit us just as they did the church in that society so many decades ago:

"For we must all appear before the judgment seat of Christ; that every one may receive the things done in his body, according to that he hath done, whether it be good or bad" (2 Cor. 5.10).

Now in the 21st century, here we are, born-again people trying to live holy lives, aiming for an increase in our faith, and eager to tell our friends and family of this wonderful experience of walking in the Spirit. We're striving to establish homes of righteous behavior where Jesus is the center of our lives. We toil over the molding of our children, giving our best as we try to inspire them to become Christians, little ones who truly love the Lord and who will grow into stalwart people of God. We're endeavoring to live up to our name—the name *Christian*—the name that means Christ-like. *Uh, Christ-like*, you say? Yes, Christ-like. It's hard, and we're struggling. But it's feasible. It's doable. God will help us. We are determined to persevere, to refuse to look back, to rally with each other, to join ranks, to link arms, to lift up ourselves and anyone else who stumbles, to learn to fully lean on God, and to trust Him in every situation. We have made a pact with ourselves and with each other. We will not fall away. We will not turn back. We will not backslide. In these next chapters, we will discuss ways to effect this resolve.

"Wherefore the rather, brethren, give diligence to make your calling and election sure: for if ye do these things, ye shall never fall: For so an entrance shall be ministered unto you abundantly into the everlasting kingdom of our Lord and Saviour Jesus Christ" (2 Pet. 1.10-11).

Chapter Eleven
Diligent Study of Scripture

Nothing will be as effective in assuring success in your Christian walk as will studying Scripture, studying to the extent that you become familiar with every story, every list of instructions, every fragment, line, and nuance, for in these pages are found the words of eternal life. The plan of salvation and the history of the church are there, as are biographies of the prophets and patriarchs. The genealogy of Jesus and the story of His birth, His death, and His glorious resurrection are there recorded. The epistles, or letters, make up most of the New Testament and were written specifically to Christians of the early church who were just learning to live for God. Even from a secular viewpoint, the Bible is regarded as some of the finest literature in the world. It is a treasure. Like no other book, the Bible is fresh every day, and although I cannot explain it, I assure you that regardless of the number of times you take that dear book into your hands, you will find that each reading will reveal anew a part of God.

Personal reading and study of the Bible is critical in the life of any Christian. Of great benefit to the new convert are structured discipleship classes that many churches offer. If you are not informed of one, ask your pastor about such a class, and promptly avail yourself of this opportunity and others of which you may learn, leaning always on recommendations from your church leaders.

Knowing the Scripture will be a source of power unlike any other you have ever known. Be aware of this advantage, and be encouraged to use this spiritual authority and weaponry. Consider that when He was tempted of satan, Jesus Himself quoted Scripture in rebuttal to the insulting words of that evil being. If it's convenient for you, please take the time right now to read in the 4th chapter of Matthew concerning this incident, in which after Jesus had fasted 40 days and nights, the devil approached and taunted Him by saying, "If Thou be the Son of

God, command that these stones be made bread" (Matt. 4.3).

The Bible does not give this detail, but I suspect those jet-brown Jewish eyes of Jesus' flashed with indignation as He whirled to face that vile being. A brilliant spectacle of a keen, well-placed blow of Scripture is found in verse 4 when Jesus said, "It is written, Man shall not live by bread alone, but by every word that proceedeth out of the mouth of God." Understand now that Jesus, while being fully God, was also fully man, so that after this period of having no food, He was very hungry and no doubt physically weak. But in this challenging moment, Jesus grasped that powerful Scripture, and as a skilled swordsman with a ready rapier, thrust it deeply into satan.

Because we are human, and because it is normal to experience emotional fluctuations, we do not depend on feelings to direct our spiritual walk. Our emotions may mislead us; indeed it is likely they will. Rather, we live by knowledge of Scripture, for Scripture is sound, sure, and unchanging. All we need to take us from this crumbling globe to that place of glorious perfection is found in God's Word:

> "All scripture is given by inspiration of God, and is profitable for doctrine, for reproof, for correction, for instruction in righteousness: That the man of God may be perfect, thoroughly furnished unto all good works" (2 Tim. 3.16-17).

Throughout the dark days that invariably come, when answers are elusive, when no way can be seen, when hopelessness is a shroud, and when we stagger as drunk men, God's Word is fixed. It is Truth. It does not waver, but is constant, ever shining with brilliant beam and with sure direction.

> "Thy word is a lamp unto my feet, and a light unto my path" (Ps. 119.105).

Chapter Twelve
~ Ardent Church Involvement ~

A s in no other agency, the opportunity to both give and to receive in the most meaningful of ways is found in one's local church. This platform for life-changing ministry is unparalleled, for it is within the framework of the church that we are drawn to God, and it is there, following our spiritual birth, that we are trained and molded. A significant note in Christian development is an urgency to tell others of this stirring experience that has changed our lives. Thus, not only have we become recipients of ministry, we are now ministers of the Gospel ourselves. Our testimony, our insight, and our view of God and the church become the basis of what we speak to our families and to our friends.

This close association and involvement with the varied facets of the church will drastically reduce our chances of falling away, for the accumulated strength and wisdom of our brothers and sisters in Christ will undergird us and will significantly contribute to our spiritual growth. This habit of coming together for worship, for training, and for evangelism may be traced throughout Scripture. Indeed, it is mandated in Hebrews 10.25. The *NIV* says it this way: "Let us not give up meeting together, as some are in the habit of doing, but let us encourage one another—and all the more as you see the day approaching." *God's Word Translation* makes it clearer yet: "We should not stop gathering together with other believers, as some of you are doing. Instead, we must continue to encourage each other even more as we see the day of the Lord coming."

1: WORSHIP

In his poetic way, David says:

"Enter into his gates with thanksgiving, and into his courts with praise: be thankful unto him and bless his name. For the LORD is good; his mercy is everlasting; and his truth endureth to all generations" (Ps. 100.4-5).

Your chances of backsliding are small if every time you enter the church your heart is full of praise. Whether your church is large or small, fancy or plain, makes no difference; it's your heart and its urge toward worshipping God that is of significance. Your hands are eager to clap (Ps. 47.1), your feet are set for dancing (Ps. 150.4), and your voice is ready for the shout (Ezra 3.11).

One who leads in worship is blessed with beautiful memories.

"These things I remember as I pour out my soul: how I used to go with the multitude, leading the procession to the house of God, with shouts of joy and thanksgiving among the festive throng" (*NIV*, Ps. 42.4).

The act of worship not only benefits me personally, bringing about emotional release and even physical healing, but sincere, whole-hearted worship conducts into the sanctuary the very presence of God Himself. Read about it here in 2 Chronicles 5.13 where praise and worship were so intense that a cloud of the presence of God filled the place:

"It came even to pass, as the trumpeters and singers were as one, to make one sound to be heard in praising and thanking the LORD; and when they lifted up their voice with the trumpets and cymbals and instruments of musick, and praised the LORD, saying, For he is good; for his mercy endureth for ever: that then the house was filled with a cloud, even the house of the LORD;"

2: Cooperation

Being enmeshed deeply in your church will not only involve worship, but will also include working closely with others. Undisputed is that working systematically and in a unified way is far superior to scattered individual efforts. The examination of the habit of birds that fly in strict formation has often been cited to convey this principle. From aerospaceweb.org, I bring this striking information:

"Persons who have studied formation flight believe that birds fly in this way for two reasons. The first reason is that the shape of the formation reduces the drag force that each bird experiences compared to if it were flying alone. This decrease in drag occurs thanks to the formation of wingtip vortices. These vortices are generally undesirable because they create a downwash that increases the induced drag on a wing in flight. However, this downwash is also accompanied by an upwash that can be beneficial to a second wing flying behind and slightly above the first.

A bird flying in one of these upwash regions essentially gains free lift so that it can fly at a lower angle of attack. As angle of attack is reduced, the induced drag is also lowered so that the bird does not need to flap its wings as hard or as often to generate the thrust needed for forward flight. Flapping the wings less often means that the bird's muscles do not work as hard and its heart rate drops. As a result, the bird does not tire as quickly and is able to fly farther.

These studies estimate that a flock of 25 birds in formation can fly as much as 70 percent further than a solo bird using the same amount of energy. Heart rates of the birds were noted to be much lower than that of the solo bird.

Even though the V formation benefits all of the birds, the bird in the lead position has to work the hardest. When this bird tires, it will drop out of the lead position and fall further back into one of the lines of the V. Another bird from further back will rapidly move forward to take the leading position and maintain the formation. The two birds in the furthest trailing positions also tire more rapidly than those in the middle so these positions are also rotated frequently to spread the most fatiguing locations throughout the flock. This cyclical rearrangement gives all birds the responsibility of being the leader as well as a chance to enjoy the maximum benefits of being in the middle of the formation. This sense of teamwork comes naturally since even the youngest members of the flock rapidly realize that it takes less work to fly in a V formation that it does to fly alone."

Recall that we are dealing with the subject of backsliding and that in this chapter we are discussing what each of us can do to avoid this tragedy. Let me once more emphasize how crucial it is that we are deeply involved with our church and with its functions, for within the church is strength and support. Within the church we learn to serve, to assist others, and to lead. We are a team—God's team. We should be drawn to the church, eager for service times, concerned for its welfare, and always striving for its growth and its prosperity.

3: ESTEEM FOR PASTOR

With highest esteem should you regard the pastor of your church. A close alliance with him will set you far on your road to heaven, for it is by scriptural authority that pastors are set as the head of the church. Christ is the ultimate Head, of course, with the pastor's headship subject to that higher One. God's heart is for pastors, for it is by Him that pastors are designated:

> "And I will give you pastors according to mine heart, which shall feed you with knowledge and understanding" (Jer. 3.15).

Not only does God speak to us through Scripture, He speaks through preachers. An account of specific direction given by God to one of His prophets is found in chapter 3 of Ezekiel verses 16 through 21. Verse 21 reads, "Nevertheless if thou warn the righteous man, that the righteous sin not, and he doth not sin, he shall surely live, because he is warned; also thou hast delivered thy soul."

God's plan for insuring our salvation in this dispensation includes preaching.

"For after that in the wisdom of God the world by wisdom knew not God, it pleased God by the foolishness of preaching to save them that believe" (1 Cor. 1.21).

"Take heed therefore unto yourselves, and to all the flock, over the which the Holy Ghost hath made you overseers, to feed the church of God, which he hath purchased with his own blood" (Acts. 20.28).

Certainly then, I should cherish, love, and highly regard my pastor. I should refuse to criticize him, remembering that he is human and thus will make mistakes. I should support him in every way, pray for him, and encourage him.

Recently I sat with a person whose pastor had likely done the local church wrong—nothing illegal or blatantly sinful—but who had taken some action that seemed unwise and that may well have a negative effect on people in the church. With silent admiration, I watched this person's facial expressions and listened to his careful words as he appropriately told of the deeds, but at the same time withheld any judgment. He spoke of closeness with his pastor and of his admiration for him. He told of the pastor's good qualities, even remarking of extenuating circumstances concerning the matter in question. He was a keen example of a saint who loves, protects, and defends his pastor.

One important caveat must be inserted here, for—unpleasant as it is to acknowledge—occasionally ministers do stray from truth. I personally know of the bewilderment and grief that arises among faithful saints who find themselves in such a predicament. Godly, righteous people whose leader has strayed from the principles of the Bible suffer intensely, for they have been taught to honor and revere their pastor, yet finally they have acknowledged the grave problem that exists. Such persons in a spirit of love and humility must seek counsel of another wise minister of the gospel. Paul was aware of this possibility when he said, "Be ye followers of me, even as I also am of Christ" (1 Cor. 11.1). I believe Paul was implicitly warning against following anyone who does not follow Christ and His teachings. Further emphasis on this point is found in the 2nd chapter of Galatians where Paul, after fourteen years, went back to Jerusalem and counseled with other leaders "…lest by any means I should run, or had run, in vain" (2.2).

In wrapping up this section, let me say once more that our intense involvement in our local churches will be of extensive value in preventing our backsliding. The love and support we give to our pastor and to those with whom we worship is of infinite value, not only to them, but also to us.

Chapter Thirteen
⟶ Understand Who You Are ⟵

1: You have been chosen by God

Within that unfathomable moment of creation, that atom of beginning time when our souls were somehow fashioned, God decided we would be His. Perhaps it was eons before our conception—who can know?—that within God's eye we were. Down the long and lingering gallery of time—or of no time, for how can we speak to our ignorance, noting that we are but creatures of time?—did He see that His Church would include us. Impossible to comprehend, is that God Himself, the creator of all, would select me. And you. Yet this gleaming truth is one we can rely on, for it is well established in Scripture. Adamantly do we claim this favored place in Him.

> "Jesus went up on a mountainside and called to Him those He wanted, and they came to Him" (NIV, Mark 3.13).
> "No man can come to me, except the Father which hath sent me draw him: and I will raise him up at the last day" (John 6.44).
> "Your eyes saw my unformed body. All the days ordained for me were written in your book before one of them came to be" (*NIV*, Ps. 139.16).

A most commanding force to guard against backsliding is this understanding that God has chosen us to be in His Kingdom. Had not God chosen us, had He not drawn us by His Spirit, we could not have been born again, baptized into His body, and regenerated. For it is only by the drawing of His Spirit that we can come to God. He chose us. As surely as He walked about Galilee handpicking disciples, so has He walked the Spirit realm and handpicked us. What honor. What opportunity.

"But ye are a chosen generation, a royal priesthood, an holy nation, a peculiar people; that ye should shew forth the praises of him who hath called you out of darkness into his marvellous light" (1 Pet. 2.9).

I love that Scripture.

2: YOU WILL ALWAYS BATTLE YOUR FLESH

An acute awareness that once we have been born again, we still must contend with our old selves, with the draw of worldliness, and with carnality, will help us avoid slipping back into sin. For while it is true that we have been filled with the Holy Ghost, it is certain that we still will grapple with temptations and with trying challenges. We are people now of two natures: one of righteousness, one of evil.

"This I say then, Walk in the Spirit, and ye shall not fulfil the lust of the flesh. For the flesh lusteth against the Spirit, and the Spirit against the flesh: and these are contrary the one to the other: so that ye cannot do the things that ye would" (Gal. 5.16-17).

To be of the mind that satan will leave us alone once we have decided to follow Jesus is a mistake. Certainly he will not, but instead may use every weapon in his arsenal to cause our spiritual death. We must be ever watchful, and while fully trusting in the staying power of the Holy Ghost, we must reckon with our humanity and with the threat of our sinful nature that at all times is eager to rise up and to again become our master. While not running scared, nor living in fear of satan and his ways, we must not forget his evil and demonic plans. Paul wrote of this concern in 2 Corinthians 2.11:

"Lest Satan should get an advantage of us: for we are not ignorant of his devices."

How wise Paul was, and how carefully should we attend his words. Let us not be ignorant of satan's ploys, but let us consider the evil that is about us as we form opinions and make plans for our lives. Let our daily steps be measured carefully, considering the guarding of our righteousness and the threat of evil snares. For out there in our very real world, as we work and play and go to school and buy groceries and put gasoline in our cars, satan is lurking.

"Be self-controlled and alert. Your enemy—the devil—prowls around like a roaring lion looking for someone to devour" (*NIV,* 1 Pet 5.8).

We must recognize and acknowledge our weaknesses, devising careful strategy for dealing with them. We must build ourselves up in the Spirit, never forgetting that we will not be saved by accident. We will be saved because we have taken advantage of every available tool, we've laid aside encumbrances, and we're fully committed to God and to His work.

Peter was the undisputed leader among the disciples, and it was to him that Jesus gave the keys of the kingdom (Matt. 16.19). Yet this powerful man of God was not immune to a satanic attack. In Luke 22.31, Jesus warned him:

"And the Lord said, Simon, Simon, behold, Satan hath desired to have you, that he may sift you as wheat:"

The devil is out to get you, Peter. Sneering, he scrutinizes you, his evil schemes as bold as lightening. No doubt, it was with keen eyes that Jesus alerted Peter of this threat and urged him to grasp this crucial concept. Scary. Scary that to this dynamic Christian Jesus should issue such a dire warning. But hang on. We are not left to nibble our fingernails in worry for that burly fisherman. No. For the next verse is a triumphant settling of our minds, not only for Peter, but also for us:

"But I have prayed for thee, that thy faith fail not: and when thou art converted, strengthen thy brethren" (Luke 22:32).

How about that! How about the thought that Jesus prayed for Peter and that when Peter finally got it all together, he would be able to strengthen his brothers. What a dynamic piece of Scripture this is, one that by logical extension and by a faithful consideration of the laws of biblical interpretation leads us to the conclusion that God also considers us, *prays* for us, and has confidence that we too will be able to resist the snare of satan.

In all areas of our lives, ultimately, decision is the key. As for me, I have decided to follow Jesus. As for me, I have decided to cut down my old sinful nature, while letting the new and righteous part of me flourish. Paul writes this way:

> "That ye put off concerning the former conversation the old man, which is corrupt according to the deceitful lusts; And be renewed in the spirit of your mind; And that ye put on the new man, which after God is created in righteousness and true holiness" (Eph. 4.22-24).

In chapter 14, we will discuss this very important issue in greater detail.

3: YOU ARE GOING TO HEAVEN

To fully grasp that we are heaven-bound is a forceful deterrent to backsliding. Think about it. We should reflect on our godly conversations and on our spiritual plans. We should peruse Scripture to be sure we are doing right, while at the same time have the understanding that despite our best efforts, we can never be good enough to go to heaven. Only through the mercy and grace of God will we make it there. But we will. We will make it. We have dedicated our lives, have purified our thoughts, and cleaned up our living. We have stumbled a time or two, but we didn't stay down. We grappled and struggled and prevailed. Heaven will be our everlasting home. Forever we will be in the presence of God. Forever we will live in paradise. We WILL make it to heaven. No sin, sickness, dialysis machines, nor wailing in the night will be part of that golden place. None. For satan will be gone, having been bound and pitched into the raging flames of the lake of fire. Neither wrenching sobs, nor desperate grasping for drugs will be known. The legs of the crippled will be straight and the eyes of the blind open. No hospital will stand on those streets of gold. No death, no dying, no sorrow. Rather, all will be glory, joy, and happiness. For Jesus, the One who redeemed us, has fashioned this spectacular place, the place called heaven, whose splendor, peace, and glory cannot be comprehended. Forever, we will abide in the presence of God. Amazing. Amazing, but true.

"For I reckon that the sufferings of this present time are not worthy to be compared with the glory which shall be revealed in us" (Rom. 8.18).

On this planet called Earth, on many occasions and for varied reasons have we cried ourselves to sleep. We have wept over our children. We have moaned for ourselves and for our weaknesses. We have bent low at caskets and flung ourselves onto grassy graves. Tormented, we raged through the night. Alone, we walked the streets of desolation and despair, our eyes running with waters of hopelessness.

Once, I sat in the car with you, you of strength, you not known for breaking down, but you, who on that day wept. You wept in terror. You wept in fear for your children. "I don't know what I'm going to do," you said, as you wiped a hand over the wet of your face. "I don't know how I can even pay the rent." But no more! You will weep no more. No tears, no terror, no hopelessness. None of that will engage us when we have made it to heaven. It will be a new day, a new place, the ultimate, that for which we have longed.

"And God shall wipe away all tears from their eyes; and there shall be no more death, neither sorrow, nor crying, neither shall there be any more pain: for the former things are passed away" (Rev. 21.4).

Although the word *rapture* is not in the Bible, within Christian circles, we often refer to the Rapture, and when we speak so, we are talking of the time when God's people will be taken away to heaven. While that particular word is not used, the event is well established in Scripture. Some refer to that rare moment as the Catching Away. Since my childhood, I have heard extensive preaching about heaven and about that miraculous time when Jesus will return to the earth for the purpose of taking His bride (that's us!) home to live with Him.

Innumerable songs about heaven have been sung. Poems have been written. I've read of people who have had visions of heaven and who have told of their perception of the glory and peace there. Others with near-death experiences have described their understanding of being in heaven and of their strong desire to stay there instead of returning to this life.

I've heard much about heaven, and I've considered it extensively. Once, in our living room many years ago, several of our friends who are ministers began talking about heaven, and although all agreed that worshipping Jesus will be our focus, the question arose as to what other activities might be involved. One of them thought we might explore the galaxies and the planets. Others smiled at the suggestion, all agreeing, I believe, that we don't know really what God has prepared for us.

Have you thought recently how it will feel as the resurrecting Spirit of God transforms us from earthlings to supernatural beings? With no pause, no lapse of moment—for time will be no more—natural laws will be suspended. The shackles of gravity will clang loose, and untethered we will rise. Over cities and the seas will we sail. Over meadows wide and mountains tall. Past the sun and the moon. Beyond the morning star and the evening star. Through the Milky Way. Past Jupiter and Mars. In a moment, it will be accomplished. In the twinkling of an eye, our life will be over, yet in the truest sense, only will it have begun. Such an event is beyond human thinking, far beyond our imagination. It is illogical and unseen. It is real. It is heaven.

"For this we say unto you by the word of the Lord, that we which are alive and remain unto the coming of the Lord shall not prevent them which are asleep. For the Lord Himself shall descend from heaven with a shout, with the voice of the archangel, and with the trump of God: and the dead in Christ shall rise first. Then we which are alive and remain shall be caught up together with them in the clouds, to meet the Lord in the air: and so shall we ever be with the Lord" (1 Thess. 4.15-17).

Such vision should keep us from drug dealers, vile imaginations, foul speech, and loose living. Let such dream undertake to turn our heads toward God, toward an altar, toward a church. May the ugly thought of backsliding be annihilated by this shimmering hope and by this wondrous expectation.

The 21st chapter of Revelation probably contains the finest description of heaven, of the New Jerusalem, to be found anywhere, and I'm encouraging you to read the entire chapter from your Bible. We have examined some of the verses already, and I have positioned a few more together here: parts of verses 2, 10-12, 18-23, and 25.

"And I John saw the holy city, new Jerusalem, coming down from God out of heaven, prepared as a bride adorned for her husband" (21.2).

"And he carried me away in the spirit to a great and high mountain, and shewed me that great city, the holy Jerusalem, descending out of heaven from God, Having the glory of God: and her light was like unto a stone most precious, even like a jasper stone, clear as crystal; And had a wall great and high, and had twelve gates …" (21.10-12).

"And the building of the wall of it was of jasper: and the city was pure gold, like unto clear glass" (21.18).

"And the foundations of the wall of the city were garnished with all manner of precious stones. The first foundation was jasper; the second, sapphire; the third, a chalcedony; the fourth, an emerald; The fifth, sardonyx; the sixth, sardius; the seventh, chrysolyte; the eighth, beryl; the ninth, a topaz; the tenth, a chrysoprasus; the eleventh, a jacinth; the twelfth, an amethyst" (21.19-20).

"And the twelve gates were twelve pearls; every several gate was of one pearl: and the street of the city was pure gold, as it were transparent glass" (21.21).

"And I saw no temple therein: for the Lord God Almighty and the Lamb are the temple of it. And the city had no need of the sun, neither of the moon, to shine in it: for the glory of God did lighten it, and the Lamb is the light thereof" (21.22-23).

"And the gates of it shall not be shut at all by day: for there shall be no night there" (21.25).

We have a grip on the matter, and we are resolved to be successful in living for God. We're understanding who we are, that Jesus bought us at great price, and that we are destined to live in heaven. God is pulling for us. He's on our side. He understands us. He is full of mercy. "Among whom also we all had our conversation in times past in the lusts of our flesh, fulfilling the desires of the flesh and of the mind; and were by nature the children of wrath, even as others. But God, who is rich in mercy, for his great love wherewith he loved us, Even when we were dead in sins, hath quickened us together with Christ, (by grace ye are saved;)" (Eph. 2.3-5).

I want to close this section by referring you to the first chapter of John, an exceptionally powerful chapter of the Bible. Read it in all its glory. Read it and revel in its truths and in its revelation. For this moment, I want to concentrate on the 12th verse, for it is pertinent to this study where we are noting that understanding who we are definitely includes the surety that heaven will be our eternal home. When we receive Him, when we receive the Holy Ghost, there is now within us supernatural power. It is God's power. Think about it. God's power now resides inside us, giving us authority and dominion, so that we go forth slaying giants and overcoming sin. Check it out here:

> "But as many as received him, to them gave he power to become the sons of God, even to them that believe on his name" (John 1.12).

Embedded in the Holy Ghost is power of the greatest extreme. Rare. Strong. Otherworldly. Interestingly, the word *power* in this verse is from the Greek word *dunamis*, which is the root of the modern English word *dynamic, dynamite,* and *dynamo.* Within our souls—we who possess the Holy Ghost—is a dynamo of power, strength, and command.

4: You are not going to hell

The assurance we are going to heaven stands on the same line—but on opposite ends—as that of the assurance that we are not going to hell. Satan would have us think otherwise, being always on the attack to sabotage our determination to live righteously. He wants to snag us and to drag us down to the pit of hell, to the pit of hell that is not intended for humans, but for the devil and his angels: "...into everlasting fire, prepared for the devil and his angels:" (Matt. 25.41). He knows his fiery destination, and among the horde of demons that will be there, he wants to add you and me. He wants us to suffer with him, to endure excruciating pain for eternity, and to be separated from the presence of God. But that will not happen, for we are God's children, and we have determined that we will not go to hell.

Do not think there is something wrong with you or with your Christian walk when satan attacks you. He stands in opposition to every person who is striving to make it to heaven. He eyed you at the moment of your spiritual birth, perhaps spat contemptuously, and deep within his disgusting mind, he purposed to stop you, to turn you back, to hinder you. Don't be surprised at his moves; just be ready. We who are singled out for satanic attacks are in good company, for recall that earlier in this book, we discussed that even Jesus was accosted by the devil. That vile creature shamelessly stood before God, who was embodied in flesh, and tempted Him.

There was a time in the Old Testament when the prophet Zechariah saw satan having the gall to stand beside the high priest. In the book of Zechariah, take a look at the first verse of chapter 3:

"And he shewed me Joshua the high priest standing before the angel of the LORD, and Satan standing at his right hand to resist him."

Talk about audacious. Boldly, into that very holy place satan strides, taking a stand right beside Joshua who was ministering. Read it again. This was no common, mundane event, for within this prophetic vision was God's priest Joshua standing before the angel of the Lord. Satan had the effrontery to push his way in with the objective of resisting the man of God. Just stood there, did satan, his sly face dripping with evil.

Lest you forget, I want to remind you that God is not unaware of those times when the devil makes his slithering moves toward us. We are never alone. We never stand defenseless. When satan seems to have disregarded every other being on the Earth and has taken us as his target for the day, remember that God knows about it. When ammunition of every caliber explodes about us and when we lie bleeding and gasping for breath, we must not lose sight of our kind, all-knowing, compassionate God. He is powerful, too, our Savior. Not only is He a loving God, He is supreme, having no peers. None should question His capability or His authority. All power in heaven and in earth is His (Matt. 28:18).

So then, as satan had weaseled his way into that holy atmosphere and stood to resist Joshua, God spoke as thunder:

> "And the LORD said unto Satan, The LORD rebuke thee, O Satan; even the LORD that hath chosen Jerusalem rebuke thee:" (Zech. 3.2).

Love it! I can see the scene as I write. How I rejoice in the understanding that God sees me, knows my every struggle, and observes the devilish attacks that threaten our families and come against our churches. God knows our young people and the depraved world in which they must exist. He understands it all.

When of a sudden, or in slimy slowness, the stench of evil pervades our places, when a hiss of corruption is hot against our ears, when deplorable phrases invade our heads and lewd vision blasts our eyes, we must stiffen in place, call up our spiritual hackles, and be aware of what is happening. With no delay, we consider that evil has invaded our ground, that beelzebub has made his moves and is threatening us with his bitter bite. Taking charge through the power of the Holy Ghost that resides in us, we will resist the evil one, the old slew foot. Our spiritual ears will be attuned to the voice of God who will unfailingly sweep in and who in His indomitable way will speak to satan: "The Lord rebuke [you]". (Zech. 3.2).

Satan will be back, though, for he knows his days are short, and that he must work fiercely during this period when he is allowed to roam about the earth. Satan will certainly work on you through your memories, condemning you for what you have done in the past, evoking visions of your compromising positions when you took part in activities that now, even at the thought, cause you shame. He is an accuser of the brethren, wanting you to be a part of those who endure eternal damnation.

> "But the fearful, and unbelieving, and the abominable, and murderers, and whoremongers, and sorcerers, and idolaters, and all liars, shall have

their part in the lake which burneth with fire and brimstone: which is the second death" (Rev. 21.8).

The future of satan is assured. His eternal destination has been long determined, and I'm happy to say, it is not pretty. Read of it here in the 12th chapter of Revelation, verses 9-10. Read about it and gloat. "And the great dragon was cast out, that old serpent, called the Devil, and Satan, which deceiveth the whole world: he was cast out into the earth, and his angels were cast out with him. And I heard a loud voice saying in heaven, Now is come salvation, and strength, and the kingdom of our God, and the power of his Christ: for the accuser of our brethren is cast down, which accused them before our God day and night."

No one should go to hell. For persons to be cast into hell is outside of the eternal plan of God, for as we have seen earlier, hell was made for the devil and for his angels. It was not with people in mind that hell was created. Hell is an awful place. It burns forever.

Forever. *Forever* is a word whose absolute and encompassing meaning is impossible for us human beings to comprehend. I understand that the most exhaustive dictionaries and the most elegant word studies have attempted such a task and that included in the effort are words such as *evermore, eternal, for good, endless, perpetual,* and the like. Yet, full comprehension is impossible, for we are but lackeys of time. We are of beginnings and endings, of life and its finish, of birth and of death.

Granted, that in such conversation I must admit to a nominal sense of forever, for I must settle with the soul issue and with my sketchy cognition of its being eternal. Such awareness, though, is of the intellect and of faith, not of experience or of observation. My taking of the subject comes from the Bible and from the Holy Ghost, with other works rounding out my perception of the soul's form.

As a child, I grappled with the question of eternity. I have clear memories of lying in bed at night and trying to grip the idea of forever, of no ending. I was not successful then, nor am I now.

Of particular distress regarding forever is thinking of those persons who will go to hell. According to the Bible, hell is a "place of torment" (Luke 16.28), of unquenchable fire (Mark 9.43), and of "outer darkness" where there is "weeping and gnashing of teeth" (Matt. 25.30).

Hell continues. "And the smoke of their torment ascendeth up forever and ever: and they have no rest day nor night, ..." (Rev. 14.11). No rest, no relief from the burning, no respite. Hell is severe. Its duration is unthinkable. The most crushing of earthly circumstances finally dissolve. The pain from a severed limb is mitigated by a narcotic and then by healing. Funerals come to an end. The agony of loss bends us double and stretches us prone on the floor, but is finally eased. We close our eyes in rest at long day's end. Our mouths wide with fearful screams are, at the last, silenced.

Not in hell. Forever it goes on.

I'm not going to hell.

Some picture God as a tyrant, sitting high over us, glaring about with eyes of steel, waiting for us to make a mistake, so He can cut us down, so He can judge us to perdition, so we will be with those who are forever tormented. This image of God is flawed. This faithless thought is in every point contrary to Scripture.

> "The Lord is not slack concerning his promise, as some men count slackness; but is longsuffering to us-ward, not willing that any should perish, but that all should come to repentance" (2 Pet. 3.9).

In direct opposition to those who would pitch God as cruel and as a tyrant before whom we should cower are these words of the great prophet Isaiah:

> "So shall they fear the name of the LORD from the west, and his glory from the rising of the sun. When the enemy shall come in like a flood, the Spirit of the LORD shall lift up a standard against him" (Isa. 59.19).

A *standard* in this sense is a flag or a banner identifying an army of warriors. In ancient battles, historians tell us, the standard-bearer would be first in the march against the enemy and the one to strike the initial bombardment. His shout would be the leading roar of the crusade. Barnes' Notes suggest, *"the Hebrew phrase from which we have the interpretation 'the Spirit of the Lord' may denote 'the wind of Yahweh' or a strong, violent, mighty wind. The appropriate signification of this word is wind or breath, and it is well known that the name of God is often used in Scripture to denote that which is mighty or vast, as in the phrase, mountains of God, cedars of God and such."*

The past several pages of this book on backsliding have dealt with thoughts of both heaven and hell. My intent is that these discourses help firm up your commitment to God and to His ways. I pray these writings will reinforce your attraction to heaven and that your disdain for satan and for hell will be fierce.

5: A WEIGHTY INFLUENCE ON YOUR CHILDREN'S DESTINY

In most cases, a parent is the strongest influence on his or her children. Whether your children go to heaven or to hell depends a great deal on you, for even though the final choice rests with the individual, most of us become like those we are around. There are exceptions, but we usually take on the values of our parents, or of those who rear us if that happens to be someone other than our biological parents. Their ethics become ours. Social skills, tastes in literature and music, educational goals, and numerous other matters reflect on our parents.

Such consideration to a conscientious Christian will be a strong impediment to thoughts of backsliding. Your babies may be small when you think of leaving the church. You are restless, lots of wild oats in your barn, and as you wrestle with the notion of turning back, you settle on the idea to be gone from the church a short while. *I know serving God is the right thing, but I don't plan to spend all my life away from God. I'll come back. I'll repent. I'll make things right.* And indeed you may, for as we have noted, God is abundantly merciful. You are His child, He loves you, and He wants you to be saved.

What, though, of your children? What of those little ones who not only push their tiny feet into your shoes and pad about the house, but who also figuratively follow in your footsteps? What of them? Can you look into their wide eyes and say, "Not going to church anymore, Baby. Just taking us a little break. I work hard on my job five days a week, attend to chores about the house on Saturday, so Sunday's my only day off. It will be okay, Baby. We'll be fine." Can you do it? Can you finger the tousled head of your five-year-old and explain there will be no more Sunday school classes, no angel roles at the church Christmas play nor bathrobed shepherds kneeling at a crooked manger? Won't your teenager be excited when you say you will not be forcing anyone to get up early on Sunday morning anymore, and that, anyway, he's old enough to decide, and maybe even the Friday night youth rallies aren't as important as we once thought. Can you say it? Can you do it?

What of the worldly events to which you would now subject your children? What of addictive habits? What of those life convictions you once regarded as wholesome (and actually still do) but that you will now by your actions disdain, and of which your children will be ignorant? How about the powerful drawing of the Holy Ghost, that supernatural anointing that despite your best efforts you cannot explain to one who hasn't felt it? What about it? What of the majestic hymns of the church whose enduring grandeur will now fall strange on the ears of your children?

The years a parent has in which to form the conscience of a child and to instill moral principles in him are of utmost consequence. Prime days are those when our children are young and when they edge hard beside us, taking in our every word and accepting our teachings as their own, our disciplines as the preferred ones. Their minds are clear. Their hearts are open. Children are saplings whose thin form and flexible bend will take to your shaping.

These paragraphs are not at all to suggest that it is only the parents who attend church who take the time to train their children and to instill principles and moral values within them. Certainly, that is not the case, for there are many parents who never go to church but who are diligent in training their children and in forming them into upright citizens of the world. It is to say, rather, that we who have fully committed our lives to Jesus will be doing our children a great disservice if we change our course. Our actions are a betrayal if we who have been filled with His Spirit, and who have elected to live a life of separation and intense service to God, move away from these dedications.

What of that return to God you planned when you left? What of coming home when you're older, when you've sown your wild oats, and when you are ready to settle back into the life you know is right? You may be able to return, for again, God is One of mercy and grace, and His arms are always reaching to you. Understand this though as you leave: your children probably will not return with you.

For they are now children of the world, having taken on its trappings and having become enmeshed in its seductions. The way of the world is theirs. A holy life separated from the world and committed to God is now strange to them, perhaps even peculiar. Why? You taught them so.

No. You will not backslide. For many reasons will you reject such temptation. Not insignificant among those reasons is the consideration of the eternal destiny of your children and of the understanding that should you make such a terrible mistake, you may well be setting your child on a downward direction that leads away from Jesus and from eternal life.

Later in this book, we will speak to an encouraging view of backsliding, that of restoration. Before we are there, though, despite the warnings I have set out here, I want to give hope and comfort to you who have backslidden and who have failed your children. I want to remind you that God wants your children to be saved and that He hears your prayers. Those godly principles you planted in your children's hearts have not been removed. The little songs they sang in Sunday school are still in their memory bank. That there were mornings when you took them by the hand and led them to church remains a fact. That on many days, for many occasions, you prayed in the Holy Ghost for them is indisputable. Heaven has record of it all.

Chapter Fourteen
Be Led by the Spirit

For several pages now we have been looking at how our personal integrity and alignment with God's plan of salvation will help us not only to avoid backsliding, but will lead us far the other way so that we are strong in Christ. Our becoming spiritually stable will not only benefit us personally but will benefit those about us, for many of those will be led to salvation because of our every day living, of our godly testimony. We've discussed such strategies as fully immersing ourselves in our local church, the study of Scripture, and in understanding who we are and where we are headed. An unexcelled tool as we strive for perfection is that of being led by the Spirit.

Being led by the Spirit is not some spooky idea indulged in by fringe groups, nor something reserved for preachers or other leaders in the church. The essence of being born again is that the Holy Ghost has come to dwell within us. God has taken up residence in an individual and is there to guide and lead that person. Again, I cannot explain how that can be, and I know it sounds illogical. Within human understanding, such a scheme is impossible. But you who have received the Holy Ghost will affirm this happening, although it is plausible that you also will have difficulty in explaining how it can be so. For we speak here of spiritual elements, not of the tangible. Our conversation extends past that of bodily concerns and so pierces that of the soul and of the mystical spirit world.

So then, once we have been born again, it is crucial that we are led by the Spirit, for we have become a new person, with fresh vision, goals, and interests. We have not left behind the natural world, but we have taken on a new dimension, having become part of another company. A forceful element has reworked us. Look at a newly born child of God, and he will appear much as before. Oh, there probably is a new gleam in his eye, perhaps even an almost physical glow about him, but his blue eyes will still be blue, his brown hair still brown, and his nose the same shape as it was previously. For a moment, though, let us suppose that somehow you were able to peel aside his skin and see his heart— not the beating one that magnificently pumps around our blood, but the one that is his soul, his innermost being. There you would clearly see astounding change. A remarkable transformation has taken place. You would now be seeing a person who is led by the Spirit.

Paul makes it abundantly clear in Romans 8.5:

"Those who live according to the sinful nature have their minds set on what that nature desires; but those who live in accordance with the Spirit have their minds set on what the Spirit desires" (*NIV*).

That new Spirit with which we have been filled is the one we will think of as we work out our lives, disregarding the sinful nature that is still a part of us, and with which we must contend as long as we are in this world. Although we have cut off the works of the flesh, our flesh is stubborn and does not easily subordinate itself. Our flesh, our sinful nature, is strong.

1: Count the cost

The benefits are sublime. They are eternal, but there definitely is a price to pay for the privilege of following Jesus. Saying we are Christian implies that our lives have changed in a drastic way. One day as He taught His disciples, Jesus spoke profoundly of the subject. Luke 9.23 records it this way:

"And he said to them all, If any man will come after me, let him deny himself, and take up his cross daily, and follow me."

A cross. Jesus knew of crosses, for He knew of His earthly destiny and that shortly He would be spiked onto one. Yes, He knew of crosses, and so He looked at those who had circled about Him, who claimed to be of Him, and said of the cross: *Take it up. Every day.*

The taking of a cross is neither of thin ornament nor of chain filigree fingered about one's neck. No. The taking of a cross implies sacrifice, suffering, and rejection. It speaks of loneliness and of pain. It speaks of eternal life.

"For whosoever will save his life shall lose it: but whosoever will lose his life for my sake, the same shall save it" (Luke. 9.24).

Strange words. Strange were many that Jesus spoke. Strange, that is, if the listener has no spiritual discernment, for it is only by the Spirit that Scripture is fully understood.

"The man without the Spirit does not accept the things that come from the Spirit of God, for they are foolishness to him, and he cannot understand them, because they are spiritually discerned" (*NIV,* 1 Cor. 2.14).

Because we do have spiritual discernment, we figure out these words that at first flush appear contradictory as regards a sensible view of human life. Jesus is making it ultimately clear that if we are to live forever—if we are to save our eternal lives—our natural man with ungodly thoughts and ambitions must die, must not be shielded. "Want to keep your life?" Jesus asked. "Then you must lose it."

In verse 25 of Luke chapter 9, Jesus graphically challenges those who listen: What sort of a decision would it be to gain the whole world and lose your soul? And again in verse 26, He emphasizes that one who refuses to bear his cross cannot be a disciple of the Lord. The decision to follow Jesus is one that should be thought out carefully, with costs honestly figured and with the nature of cross-bearing fairly calculated. Please give more thought to this subject, and read in your Bible through verse 30.

2: CONSTANT PRUNING

Let me tell you of an oak tree that once stood on our lawn here in Crestline. It was large, healthy, and beautiful. But there were too many trees in our yard, and in an undesirable way, the large limbs of this particular one was growing into those of another great oak. In addition, the tree in question obstructed a magnificent view of sky, mountains, and trees that could be seen through our dining room window. Though we are both fond of trees, Jerry and I agreed that the tree should be removed, and it was cut down. That great oak was sawed into pieces, chopped at, pitched into a wood box, carried onto our hearth, and finally burned in our fireplace. Its massive stump, though, remains—a stump that refuses to die.

From that stump, year round, grow beautiful green leaves and healthy oak tree shoots. That tree has never given up, never submitted, never surrendered. Every few months, Jerry gets out there with choppers of some kind and whacks away at the growth that refuses to quit growing. He grumbles and hacks away. And does it again.

So it is with our carnal nature. We have cut it down, whacked away the limbs of sinfulness, and for a while, they do not trouble us. Before long, though, shoots are sprouting from that massive trunk that has not died and with which we must contend. We feel the prickle of the limb as it urges us back into sin and iniquity.

Paul tells us what to do about the problem as he writes to the Galatians in chapter 5, verse 16. He speaks in a practical way, and with specificity, concerning the difference of walking in the flesh and of walking in the Spirit. If you walk in the Spirit, he teaches, you will not give in to your flesh:

"This I say then, Walk in the Spirit, and ye shall not fulfil the lust of the flesh" (Gal. 5.16).

In verse 17, he warns of the battle that we all face, the battle between good and evil, between God and satan, between flesh and Spirit:

"For the flesh lusteth against the Spirit, and the Spirit against the flesh: and these are contrary the one to the other: so that ye cannot do the things that ye would."

Once we have been filled with the Holy Ghost and we have committed to this walk in the Spirit, we will drastically change our lives. The severe alteration in our spiritual bent will affect us in every way. Our emotions, our desires, our thinking, and our activities will be radically revised. It strikes me as peculiar that people can go to church on Sunday, pious and prayerful, bearing the trappings of a Christian, and on Monday revert to thoughts and actions that bespeak a carnal nature and that inevitably produce works of the flesh. If our behavior is such, one may question whether or not we have truly been born again. For in verses 19-21 of Galatians chapter 5 Paul names some works of the flesh, ending with the words "they which do such things shall not inherit the kingdom of God."

Now these terse sayings by Paul are not denominational words. They are neither Baptist, nor Pentecostal, nor Presbyterian. They are biblical. They are the Word of God, and by His Word we will be judged.

Check it out here, or better yet, grab your own Bible and beginning with verse 19, read it for yourself:

"Now the works of the flesh are manifest, which are these; Adultery, fornication, uncleanness, lasciviousness, Idolatry, witchcraft, hatred, variance, emulations, wrath, strife, seditions, heresies, Envyings, murders, drunkenness, revellings, and such like: ..."

Go ahead now and read again verse 21 where Paul warns that if we do such things, we will not inherit the kingdom of God; we are not going to heaven. Verse 24 is also a strong one, saying that if we are Christ's, we will have "crucified the flesh." We will have cut off worldly affections and will lust no more for them.

To those who have recently been born again, this seems a good place to say that you should not linger in taking these steps. Do not hesitate. Look about you. Consider the appearance of those godly men and women who should now be your role models. Emulate them. Hear God's voice as he convicts you of your former way of dress and of talk. Look about you. Listen carefully.

3: Recall Scripture

There is so much to know about God, and even those who have served Him for many years are always learning, for who can plumb the depth of His great love, or who can fully comprehend His wide plan? Being led by the Spirit is as though God takes us personally by the hand and ushers us into a private garden where we sit and commune together. He speaks wisdom and shares insight. When we read His Word, blinders fall from our eyes, and our hearing becomes acute. Indeed all our natural senses are heightened as we walk in the Spirit. The Holy Ghost is teaching us.

> "Which things also we speak, not in the words which man's wisdom teacheth, but which the Holy Ghost teacheth; comparing spiritual things with spiritual" (1 Cor. 2.13).

It excites me to see newly developing children of God as they experience the thrill of being led by the Spirit. These new babies in Christ usually have little knowledge of Scripture, yet often as they try to explain to others what has happened in their lives, they will find their minds to have become sharpened in a most dramatic fashion. Pertinent verses of Scripture they have read only in a cursory way may be brought to their memory as they speak of their new life in Christ. In John 14.25 and 26 we read Jesus' own words concerning this phenomenon:

> "These things have I spoken unto you, being yet present with you. But the Comforter, which is the Holy Ghost, whom the Father will send in my name, he shall teach you all things, and bring all things to your remembrance, whatsoever I have said unto you."

Got it? Jesus is reminding His disciples that after He has gone away to heaven those principles He has personally taught them will be brought again to their memory through their walking in the Spirit. Walking with Jesus is such a thrilling life. To think that the Holy Ghost may quicken our little minds so that we can share the good news of the Gospel with our loved ones is truly amazing.

4: Equip for battle

This walking in the Spirit entails more than sweet visits with Jesus in a garden, but also calls up battle and fighting. In Ephesians chapter 6 we have Paul's renowned call to arms along with his description of the armor with which a child of God must be outfitted. Paul is in prison as he writes these remarkable words.

Verse 10 concludes, "Finally my brethren, be strong in the Lord, and in the power of his might." In our society today, where strength of character is little seen, and where serving God is often judged as soft and wimpy, each of us needs to take Paul's words as being pointed our way, directed to each of us personally. This is a day that calls for men and women to be strong in the Lord. We need to step up boldly and operate in the power of His might, never forgetting that God's strength surpasses the most powerful of dynamos, the most formidable arsenals. If we let His power work through us as His Spirit leads us, we can effect miracles such as might never be imagined. A person thought most unlikely and unaccomplished may be the one God will use to spark revival in your church. Yours may be the church that drastically alters its community, changing that of empty weak churches to buildings crammed with people who are experiencing Holy Ghost revival.

As I wrote this afternoon, I was reminded of the ministry of Charles Finney, born in 1792, a descendent of Puritans. From a biography written by J. Gilchrist Lawson and posted at gospeltruth.net/lawsonbio. htm is Rev. Finney's own account of his conversion:

"But as I turned and was about to take a seat by the fire, I received a mighty baptism of the Holy Ghost. Without any expectation of it, without ever having the thought in my mind that there was any such thing for me, without any recollection that I had ever heard the thing mentioned by any person in the world, the Holy Ghost descended on me in a manner that seemed to go through me, body and soul …No words can express the wonderful love that was shed abroad in my heart. I wept aloud with joy and love; and I do not know but I should say, I literally bellowed out the unutterable gushings of my heart."

Charles Finney's biographer continues:

"Sometimes the power of God was so manifest in his meetings that almost the entire audience fell on their knees in prayer or were prostrated on the floor. Sinners were often brought under conviction of sin almost as soon as they entered these cities. Finney seemed so anointed with the Holy Spirit that people were often brought under conviction of sin just by looking at him. When holding meetings at Utica, New York, he visited a large factory there and was looking at the machinery. At the sight of him one of the operatives, and then another, and then another broke down and wept under a sense of their sins, and finally so many were sobbing and weeping that the machinery had to be stopped while Finney pointed them to Christ."

Amazing. God help us. In what may be the final days of this dispensation, I pray that God will guide our leaders into action that will produce an unrestrained tide of Holy Ghost revival, a revival that will virtually inundate our country with His manifest Spirit. As I engaged in the final editing of this book, I was thrilled to learn of a Holy Ghost outpouring in a Memphis, TN *Cracker Barrel* restaurant. On Facebook.com is Gerald Depew's account:

"An amazing event happened June 25, 2011 at the Cracker Barrel in Memphis. While Pentecostals were eating dinner, the Holy Ghost moved on an employee. She desired to be filled with the Holy Ghost. She was brought to me by Tracy Cochran. This employee received the Holy Ghost and this started a chain reaction. Others wanted this gift also. Eight received the Holy Ghost!!!"

I submit that such happenings come about because of spiritual hunger that has led to the donning of the full armor of God. Realistically expecting devilish onslaughts and hellish resistance, we at the same moment know there are multitudes of people around us who want to know God and who are being awakened to their need of a Savior. We prepare ourselves for such opportunity.

Beginning in verse 11 of Ephesians chapter 6, Paul says:

"Put on the whole armor of God, that ye may be able to stand against the wiles of the devil. For we wrestle not against flesh and blood, but against principalities, against powers, against the rulers of the darkness of this world, against spiritual wickedness in high places."

It has been said many times, but it seems good to repeat it here: sometimes we should do nothing, except stand. Stand still. Flex your spiritual muscles, but don't move. Situations may arise for which, to our minds, there is no viable solution, and about which even after we have prayed, we do not know what to do. We are troubled. We are perplexed. These are times when we need to camp right here on the words of Paul:

"Wherefore take unto you the whole armor of God, that ye may be able to withstand in the evil day, and having done all, to stand" (Eph. 6.13).

Stand. We must just stand. We are living right. We are outfitted with the armor of God, and we are headed in the right direction. This is not the time to dash about in a haphazard way while recklessly making decisions. Such ill-advised actions often lead to chaotic homes where little of the peace of God is felt, children are confused, and family order is disrupted. Sadly, our society is one of careening about, of racing down freeways, through city streets, and over small town byways. A frantic sense of urgency hangs about us churning out the feeling that we must always be full-tilt ahead. Stop. Stand. Listen. Listen to the Spirit that will lead you. Don't hear anything right now? Keep standing. Keep listening.

Beginning in verse 14, Paul delves further into descriptions of this armament. Take out your Bible and read every word of this important passage. Study it closely. Have a few friends over to sit around your living room while analyzing these important Christian military instructions. Chief points and names of the gear are as follows:

- Belt of truth buckled around your waist (Verse 14)
- Chest covered with breastplate of righteousness (Verse 14)
- Feet slipped into shoes made with the preparation of the Gospel (Verse 15)

- Shield of faith at the ready (Verse 16)
- Helmet of salvation covering your head (Verse 17)
- Sword of the Spirit, the Bible, grasped firmly in your hand (Verse 17)

I want to go on to verse 19 before we finish our study here, for the ending words of Paul are riveting, containing a piece of information that we must not overlook. If you are reading here with a true desire to walk in the Spirit, there is a strong possibility that you will be gripped by great passion for the work of God as you consider the writer of these stimulating words.

Paul is speaking here:

"Pray also for me, that whenever I open my mouth, words may be given me so that I will fearlessly make known the mystery of the gospel. For which I am an ambassador in chains. Pray that I may declare it fearlessly, as I should" (*NIV,* Eph. 6.19-20).

God had chosen Paul for a mighty work, although Paul was so misguided that before God stopped him, he had gone about the land persecuting Christians, even to the extent that he was among the crowd that watched as Stephen was stoned to death. But God had plans for Paul and wanted him in His kingdom. One day, as Paul journeyed to Damascus, God literally struck him down in the middle of the road, revealing Himself in a most unusual way. Read the whole story of Paul's conversion in the 9th chapter of Acts.

Although he had earlier been a fierce opponent of Christians and had actively engaged in their persecution, after that unusual experience on the Damascus Road and the ones during the following days, Paul became a mighty man for God, a powerful force in the early church. Had we considered his earlier activities, we might have judged unlikely his becoming that revered apostolic man who in such a profound way helped establish the early church. Paul speaks of himself as being unimpressive, not only in physical appearance, but also in speaking ability (2 Cor. 10.10). As an aside, though, we may wonder if these words of Paul speak to his humility, considering the occasion in Lystra when after hearing him speak, the listeners cried, "...The gods are come down to us in the likeness of men" (Acts 14.11).

More than once during his years of remarkable ministry, Paul was arrested and thrown into jail. Bible scholars believe he spent five to six years in prison, and that during those times, he wrote entire books of the New Testament. It was during one of these stints that he wrote the passage we have been studying. Now, look again at Ephesians 6, verses 19 and 20. This dear man who was so mightily used by God speaks here of his deep emotions, revealing that despite the hand of God being on him in such a forceful way, there were moments that he was troubled in much the same as are any of us. Immediately following that masterful description of the armor of God and after his call to God's people to be so outfitted, he makes a personal plea: *Pray for me. I don't want to be afraid. I want to speak God's Words, yet I am in chains.*

After his final arrest, Paul was returned to Rome where under Nero's reign, he was martyred. That great apostle was either beheaded or, in an arena, torn apart by wild animals before a cheering crowd. *Pray for me,* he pled in his writings. *Pray that I will be fearless in proclaiming the truth of God.*

What example. What power. What effectiveness.

5: Especially guard your mind

As we continue to address this crucial issue of being led by the Spirit, I want to point out that while satan may attack your body to thwart your living a holy life, more likely is that he will attack your mind. While we should not live in fear of the devil, as we have studied before, we need to be aware of his devices and should at all times be prepared for his onslaught. During these times of attack on our minds, we must ensure we have on our heads the helmet of salvation. We are prepared and understand 2 Corinthians 10.5 which says,

"We demolish arguments and every pretension that sets itself up against the knowledge of God, and we take captive every thought to make it obedient to Christ" (NIV).

We do not consider contrary ideas that come into our minds; rather, we rout them from our intellect. We take charge of our minds. We make our every thought become obedient to the thoughts of Jesus, to the guidelines of Scripture, to living a holy and righteous life. We simply ignore those arguments unbelievers may use to dissuade us. For anything that sets itself against the knowledge of God is not working to our benefit; rather, it seeks our downfall.

If you have not yet memorized this next Scripture, this would be a good day to do so, for any of us would be hard-pressed to find another piece of writing that is so apt regarding what we should do with our minds.

> "Finally, brethren, whatsoever things are true, whatsoever things are honest, whatsoever things are just, whatsoever things are pure, whatsoever things are lovely, whatsoever things are of good report; if there be any virtue, and if there be any praise, think on these things" (Phil. 4.8).

Is that not the greatest Scripture, so beautifully written and yet so practical? You might want to sit down with your children and help them understand how crucial it is that they guard their thoughts. Repeated filling of their minds with images of violence and debauchery, whether from a television screen, a video game, or any other source, is hardly guarding their minds. Rather, it is opening those impressionable consciences to careless regard of such activities, a turning of the head, an excusing of the behavior.

We become as those with whom we run. We take on their values, visit their places, drink the cup they offer, and eat the food of their plate. Be wise.

We become what we hear. We become what we see. Choose carefully. Select judiciously, for it is your destiny. It is your future.

6: DOERS OF THE WORD

My final word here on being led by the Spirit attends to earlier text and will underscore the belief that to thrive, a Christian must acknowledge every principle of God. To distinctly walk in the Spirit so that we avoid backsliding, without reservation, we must vigilantly regard every counsel of spiritual unction. We must overlook nothing. I have written of intense study of Scripture and of the power of anointed preaching, and it is that platform I want to augment.

No amount of Bible study will prevent our backsliding unless we heed the lines therein. We may have memorized treasured portions and underlined significant verses. We may revel in their poetic element and in their profound truths, but if we do not as the Word says, our markings are as vapor and our memory as but the wind.

Our shelves may press tight with audio and video capture of the ministry of our favorite preachers. But though God chose preaching to save believers (1 Cor. 1.21), if those anointed words are not allowed to do their work within us, our listening is but vanity, futility.

"For if any be a hearer of the word, and not a doer, he is like unto a man beholding his natural face in a glass: For he beholdeth himself, and goeth his way, and straightway forgetteth what manner of man he was" (Jas. 1.23-24).

We must go well past our daily Bible reading and the workbooks in our discipleship classes. We must move beyond the comfort we feel as we sit together in worship and as we listen to God's men preach and teach. An oracle of God they have become, and we know it. We revel in it. We feel it. We must, though, push ourselves past those moments, for not only must we read and listen, we must hear in the most elevated way. We hear and we do. We are not hearers only, but we are doers.

Instruction has come that will keep us settled, that will assure our feet is on the narrow way that leads to heaven, but we must attend to what we hear. Becoming students of Scripture is imperative so that we will fill our minds with God's principles and instructions for righteousness. We must train our children in all His ways, fiercely guarding our homes, and with care discern what will be allowed within its walls. Prayer meetings at the church should not find us absent. The sound of prayer in our homes should not be foreign or awkwardly marked. Consistent and honest tithing should be routinely handled, as should be joyful giving. Our homes should be of peace, a steady light in our neighborhoods. We should be loyal members of our church, engaging in an evangelistic lifestyle in which we often lead others to Jesus Christ.

Moses had died, and God had selected Joshua to be the leader of the Israelites. Although this account was of generations ago, and took place in a radically different culture from ours, there are marked similarities, and there is relevant instruction for us today. This portion of Scripture may be a bit lengthy for our format here, but please indulge me and dig in a little, for I believe you will find it of great benefit. I draw this parallel: As the Israelites stood on the brink of entering into the land that had long ago been promised them, so we stand today, doubtless on the brink of the coming of Jesus when we will enter heaven, our promised land. With this in mind, please read the following words.

"After the death of Moses the servant of the Lord, the Lord said to Joshua son of Nun, Moses' aide: 'Moses my servant is dead. Now then, you and all these people, get ready to cross the Jordan River into the land I am about to give to them—to the Israelites. I will give you every place where you set your foot, as I promised Moses. Your territory will extend from the desert to Lebanon, and from the great river, the Euphrates—all the Hittite country—to the Great Sea on the west" (*NIV*, Josh. 1.1-4).

God's promise of dominion is as applicable to us today as it was when He spoke these words through His servant Joshua. Those Israelites who stood on the brink of Jordan were about to see that mighty river rolled up into a heap. As those millions of God's people crossed into Jericho, the riverbed would be stone dry. Though we do not stand on a physical riverbank today, the principle is the same, and the promise of dominion is extended to us. Let's continue with the story.

"No one will be able to stand up against you all the days of your life. As I was with Moses, so I will be with you; I will never leave you nor forsake you. Be strong and courageous, because you will lead these people to inherit the land I swore to their forefathers to give them" (*NIV*, Josh. 1.5-6).

I want to encourage you today, you who read here, you who have your eyes set on heaven, you who struggle, you who have fallen and have risen and have fallen and have risen again. You. I want to remind you of the power of the Holy Ghost you have and that as desperate as your situation may seem—not only seem, but be—no one can stand against you. For we do not stand alone. We have not been abandoned. We are not forsaken. Jesus said He would never leave us nor would He forsake us. Be strong and courageous is my message to you today.

"Be strong and very courageous. Be careful to obey all the law my servant Moses gave you; do not turn from it to the right or to the left, that you may be successful wherever you go." Do not let this Book of the Law depart from your mouth; meditate on it day and night, so that you may be careful to do everything written in it. Then you will be prosperous and successful" (*NIV,* Josh. 1.7-8).

The Word of God. The Scripture. Don't forget about it, don't stop quoting it, remember its laws, and don't depart from them. In closing here, I want to emphasize this measure of Scripture where Joshua has astutely called for obedience to God's Word.

"Be careful that you do everything written in it." (*NIV*, Josh. 1.8).

THE TAPPING

I sat in the auditorium of Pipkin Junior High School in Springfield, MO, where I was either in the 7th or 8th grade. The lights had been dimmed so that the room was dark. I waited.

Pipkin must have been a cutting-edge school, for this was an event sponsored by a sorority, and even to me now, it seems unusual for a junior high school to have fraternity and sorority groups. But it did, and on this day in the early '50s, I waited, as did the hundreds of others in the darkened auditorium. There had been music and announcements, and now the stage was set—set for the tapping.

The tapping was done with a wand, sparkly and fashioned as a star. Somewhere in that dimmed space, a young woman, already a member of the sorority, was moving about to make the selections. In a private meeting, a few girls had been chosen to be new members and, any minute now, would be tapped. With an easy move, the fairy wand would touch the head of each chosen girl, and she would know of her honor.

I waited, hoping I would be chosen. But I was not selected, and soon the program was over. The lights came up, and we walked from the auditorium. I was deeply disappointed.

What I didn't reckon with then, when I was 12 or 13 years old, was that already I had been tapped. Already, I had been chosen. Jesus had come by my place, had knocked gently on my heart, and had inducted me into the highest organization known to man—the Church of the Living God.

Chapter Fifteen
~ *Separation* ~

A discussion of separation is fitting to a work on backsliding, for an understanding that the Christian life is distinctive and involves being set-apart is crucial if one is to embrace such a way of living. Without a definite divorcement from the world, every Christian is in danger of backsliding.

Unfortunately, in many circles, the term *separation from the world* has taken on a negative connotation so that when the subject is discussed, an unenthusiastic mood may develop. Defensive walls are commonly thrown up, and if one looks closely, a slight rolling of the eye may be seen. Spirits bristle. If we think coherently about this issue, though, and if we analyze the arguments as positioned beside the Word of God, we might well consider these contrary responses to be unreasoned and illogical.

In the first place, the teaching of separation comes directly from the Bible.

"Therefore, come out from among unbelievers, and separate yourselves from them, says the LORD. Don't touch their filthy things, and I will welcome you " (*New Living Translation,* 2 Cor. 6.17).

These are Paul's words to one of the early church congregations, and it is fair to view this verse as being a biblical mandate. In consideration of that, we as Christians don't have a choice. Paul didn't say you might evaluate this, might think about it, or it might be a wise move. No. Rather, this is clearly an instruction to those newly established Christians and, by extension, to us in this 21st century church.

Why should we kick against such directive? How is it that we would dig in our heels and resist these words of Paul? Are we not changed? Do we not now have different desires and ambitions? Why would we choose otherwise? As born-again believers, we have now taken on the attributes of Christ so that no longer do the trappings of the world entice us. Filthy language is repulsive. Suggestive and lewd metaphors fall uneasily on our ears. The smoky environs of taverns and saloons seem inappropriate gathering spots now, and it is hard to think of conversing in a cocktail lounge with our friends about the Wednesday night Bible study class or the next youth rally. *And that cross.* Remember the cross we have taken up, the one Jesus said we must bear if we are to be His followers? Remember? Will that cross on my shoulder even let me pass through the doorway of such a place, or will it hang there, jolting me and causing me to remember who I am?

Separate yourselves, says the Word. If we are to see this mandate in the favorable light to which it easily lends itself, we need to think of the joy of separation. This separation is a step up. It is beauty and honor and fellowship with God and with His people. Separation is freedom, of bondage left behind, of broken chains. Separation from the world does not leave us desolate and bereft; rather, we have turned about and are now facing a new direction. We are separated to God. He stands beside us. We are circled about with new family, with the family of God.

My last few hours of reflection and study of separation have led me to Jeremiah 15.17 where that great Old Testament prophet speaks to this issue:

> "I never sat in the company of revelers, never made merry with them; I sat alone because your hand was on me …" (*NIV*).

Here it is. Here is the gist of the matter, the understanding I hope we can fully grasp at this very moment, for it is a crucial thought. We are separate not because it is a punishment of a tyrannical god who wants us miserable and ugly. We are not separated on mere whim of a deity. Our pastors are not severe because of teaching this principle. Not at all. Quite the opposite is true, for we are the exceptional ones, those of elevation, those of advancement and of preference. We have been called out, called forth, illuminated; we are that city set on a hill (Matt. 5.14). *We are mandated to separation from the world **because God's hand is on us!***

Well did Jeremiah understand this, for it was of divine influence that sheer ecstasy came over him and anointed him to write. The hand of

Jehovah touched Jeremiah. He reached for parchment. He reached for a pen to begin scribing those godly visions. He was called. He knew it, and to this calling, Jeremiah devoted his entire life. Often he sat alone—because the hand of God was on him. The eternal One communed with him. The essence of He who is without beginning or without ending filled the room where in silence Jeremiah sat. The Almighty was there. With little difficulty, then, do I comprehend Jeremiah's saying, *I didn't make merry with them today, didn't join in their revelings…because God's hand was on me* (15.17).

When God's hand is on us so that our mode of living drastically changes, our new way is beautiful and is one of strength. Taken from Isaiah's writings are these words:

> "Awake, awake; put on thy strength, O Zion; put on thy beautiful garments …Break forth into joy, sing together," (Isa. 52.1 and 9).

The modest clothing and demeanor of the righteous are beautiful garments, and we wear them gladly. With no condemnation do we walk about, nor do we feel inappropriately covered as we kneel in the presence of God. We are joyful. We break forth into song. For we are the set apart ones; we are the chosen who walk with God. By way of God's direction, we have removed ourselves from that of corruption and of immorality.

> "Depart ye, depart ye, go ye out from thence, touch no unclean thing; go ye out of the midst of her; be ye clean, that bear the vessels of the LORD" (Isa. 52.11).

Some people make the mistake of trying to be a Christian while at the same time attempting to maintain a worldly identification. Half-turned, they stand in the doorway to God's sanctuary. This is an untenable position that without correction inevitably leads to backsliding, for we cannot be both of the world and of God. We cannot serve two masters (Matt. 6.24). Open your Bible and read it there. We will either love one or the other—not both, for we cannot declare a neutral position. If we love one, we will hate the other. We cannot be of two minds. The book of James is emphatic about this:

"You adulterous people, don't you know that friendship with the world is hatred toward God? Anyone who chooses to be a friend of the world becomes an enemy of God" (*NIV*, Jas. 4.4).

I don't want to be an enemy of God. I don't want to turn toward the world with its traps and its ugliness. I want God's people to be my friends. I want to pray with them, to have parties in their homes, and to be joyful as we sing and revel in the Spirit of God.

Of the righteous do I want to take counsel. Of their style will I mold myself, for it is fitting to do so. God mandates it. It is His Word.

"The Lord spoke to me with His strong hand upon me, warning me not to follow the way of this people. He said: 'Do not call conspiracy everything that these people call conspiracy; do not fear what they fear, and do not dread it'" (*NIV*, Isa. 8.11-12).

How foolish, God was saying, is it to follow the trends and the thinking of the world.

Satan is a deceiver, and the walls of the church do not keep him away. Give beelzebub his due, I suppose, for in many people's minds, he has been able to manipulate this idea of separation, turning it from a model of beauty into one of dread. Rather than comprehending the design of God within that noble philosophy, those persons have taken up the notion that separation is of chains and of bondage. Hear me if you are listening to such words: That is the voice of satan. Those ideas spring from his wickedness and from his evil deceit. Separating ourselves from the world is not of bondage; rather, it takes us into the relationship of a loving father and his child. In our sinful state, we had no right to God, but now through the spirit of adoption, we are able to call God our Father:

"For ye have not received the spirit of bondage again to fear; but ye have received the Spirit of adoption, whereby we cry, Abba, Father" (Rom. 8.15).

To illuminate the wisdom of Christians who refrain from looking to ungodly persons as patterns for their lives, I remind you of three pertinent developments:

In the mid 1990s, the Oval Office of the White House in Washington, D. C. suffered obscene desecration by the man who, by earthly standards, held the highest position in the world.

The news broke recently that the immediate past governor of California has revealed the existence of a child born a few years ago as a result of his adulterous relationship with one of the housekeepers where he and his wife lived. Before he was governor, this man was a movie star. He served as model—a role model for the world.

On my computer screen as I write this is an account of a movie being shown at the Cannes Film Festival. Called *The Skin I Live In,* the story is of a mad surgeon whose daughter had been raped, and who, because of the trauma in her life, had committed suicide. Her father took the rapist to an operating chamber, gave him a sex change, and then transplanted his deceased daughter's face onto the rapist's body. Later, the surgeon had sex with the man he had turned into a woman—a woman that now bore the face of his daughter. This account is so vile and so morbid that many horrified viewers— to their credit—walked out from the showing. Listen to this, though: others, at the conclusion of the film, gave the producer a five-minute standing ovation. The critics love the film, and it is being placed in contention for the highest Cannes honor. Our newspapers are filled with similar accounts every day, the media replete with disgusting news. It is sickening.

What then? Should we take counsel of such authority? Should we style our clothing by their pattern? Should we model our lives by theirs? Should their opinions count toward the parting manner or the length of my hair? Should their style determine the fit of my sons' trousers? The question is the epitome of silliness, but of such essence is the often muttered view that to come out from among the world and to be separate smacks of legalism, of bondage, of backwardness.

But oh, these wise words of Isaiah:

"The Lord Almighty is the one you are to regard as holy, he is the one you are to fear, he is the one you are to dread, and he will be a sanctuary" (*NIV,* 8.13).

How can I go wrong if I follow after God, if I search out His precepts, if I long for His understanding and His blessing? He is holy, and He will be my sanctuary, my rest, and my peace.

To no better place will I point my children than to the church. No better role models can I select than those godly men and women who are striving to be like Jesus. Those imperfect ones. The ones who make mistakes. The ones who are sincere and who read the Bible to discern their ways and to route their paths. The ones who take their babies for anointing when they're sick and who point to the man standing in that sacred place and say, "That's your pastor, Baby. Love him. Listen to him. Pray for him." The ones whose god is not their pitiful possessions nor their high stack of coins. The ones who are modest and who speak with care. The ones who love and who laugh. Those are the models I have chosen. To those I point today. It is the joy and beauty of separation I recommend.

What of you? Across whose line will you step? Will it be to the world, or will it be to God? To decline to decide is to decide.

"Elijah went before the people and said, 'How long will you waver between two opinions? If the LORD is God, follow him; but if Baal is God, follow him.' But the people said nothing" (*NIV*, 1 Kings 18.21).

Both very sad and quite disturbing is also this scripture:

"Even while these people were worshiping the LORD, they were serving their idols. To this day their children and grandchildren continue to do as their fathers did" (*NIV*, 2 Kings 17.41).

Here is an account of people who thought they could serve both the world and God. The tragic outcome is that for generations, their children continued in their faulty ways. Those parents taught their children to turn their backs on God. They played at church, pretending to be righteous, while at the same time bowing to their idols. They taught well their children, whose own idols were in turn petted and whose sin continued.

A few with such mindset may read here today. If so, I am sad for you. For without question, no amount of Scripture will convince one who has closed ears and who has eyes that refuse to see. How wise are we to unclench our fists, to let down those walls, to let Jesus in.

I've taken up camp with those who sincerely strive after God. With honest hearts, we determine to live righteous lives that will take us to heaven. Thus, we take instruction. When we sit down together, open our Bibles, and study, it is a holy undertaking, and we may be both blessed and challenged. We want to know truth, so we have taken down any walls that might hinder our understanding. We want to be sure of our salvation, so we heed the verse that points to working out our own salvation with fear and trembling (Phil. 2.12). Working out our salvation "with fear and trembling" leaves no room for defensiveness, nor does it allow for the covering of holes in our arguments, nor of flawed logic, except for those times when faith must have its head. In our times of such seeking and such trembling, our fists loose their grip on what may have been long-held contentions. The church across the way may hold to certain tenets that once we held as ours, but truthful introspection acknowledges such platform as not being biblical. Because we are sincere, because we want to be sure of making it to heaven, we make consecrations we had not planned. We separate ourselves from places we in times past attended. We teach our eyes to see that which is righteous and our ears to listen for the holy. Our bodies are regarded as the temple of God, and to that end, we attire them. We no longer take direction from the world but from God and from His Word. With joy have we separated ourselves from the world. The benefits are amazing, unspeakable, and of another world.

One last point around separation is that such action should never be of exclusiveness or of haughtiness. Rather, separation lovingly draws lines where with non-judgmental attitudes we disassociate ourselves from venues where sin is elevated. We spend less time with those whose life-style is in complete opposition to God and to His principles, obviously leading to the building of new friendships among those who have similar interests and worldview.

This coming out from the world and separating ourselves is certainly not of communes, nor of lifting our skirts to step high over those less fortunate. When we are separated from the world because God's hand is on us, we are eager to share the Gospel with those who haven't yet heard how wonderful it is. Joyfully, we tell our friends and families of the glory of the separated life.

Chapter Sixteen
~ The Dirt Problem ~

*N*ever *seen anything like it,* they were saying, and even though that one called John had told some whopping stories, who was to know the end of this plot, and, anyway, John was now in prison, so maybe he didn't even know what he was talking about. But the phenomenon continued, and smack in the rut of dirt paths and in the watering spots of the villages and in the back rooms of tiny houses, Jesus spoke, and touched people, and miracles flared. Red-hot faces paled as scalding fevers cooled. Litters were cast away as invalids leaped free, strong and straight-limbed.

I'll take you and you, Jesus said. *Leave your nets,* and on the Sabbath day, they followed Him as He walked through the clapping doors of the synagogue and taught. Within the sanctuary, as an unclean spirit raged and tore his victim, the man cried out. Jesus spoke. *Be quiet. Come out of him.* Wounded by violent seizure, the man shuddered, free now, and quiet. Lifting his eyes, tormented no longer, he gazed into the face of Jesus and "...they were all amazed ..." (Mark 1.27).

As wildfire licks its hot tongue over withered field, consuming all in its way, so did the fame of Jesus sweep across the small parched land of Palestine. *Messiah. Where are you, Messiah? We're thirsty; we need you.* Some had understanding and knew Him, recognizing Him to be their Lord. Others were blinded and continued their search. But multitudes came, for His fame spread throughout the land.

One day, He began to speak at the edge of the water, but the crowd was enormous and someone judged there were just too many people for Jesus to teach effectively. An unnamed man brought a boat and helped the Master into it. They rowed the boat a short distance out, probably to take advantage of the amplification of sound over the water, and from a simple vessel in the swaying sea, Jesus taught a lesson, a profound lesson of ground, of dirt. It has to do with backsliding.

"Harken; Behold, there went out a sower to sow: And it came to pass, as he sowed, some fell by the way side, and the fowls of the air came and devoured it up. And some fell on stony ground, where it had not much earth; and immediately it sprang up, because it had no depth of earth: But when the sun was up, it was scorched; and because it had no root, it withered away. And some fell among thorns, and the thorns grew up, and choked it, and it yielded no fruit. And other fell on good ground, and did yield fruit that sprang up and increased; and brought forth, some thirty, and some sixty, and some an hundred" (Mark. 4.3-8).

To be aware that no matter how careful we are to avoid offense, and how watchful we are of the souls of those around us, many of them will backslide anyway is heartrending. We just will not be effective in preventing this. Whoa! you say. How can that be? Well, the lesson comes from Jesus, the One who taught of dirt and its significance, so we must delve into His words and sort through their meanings. I admit that, for me, this is a difficult passage, for my underlying question is can anyone change his dirt style?

I'm not the only one to seek further understanding of this teaching of Jesus, for, once, when He was alone with His disciples, one of them asked, *Uh, Jesus, now what is this You are saying about dirt? This talk of soil types, of stones, roots, thorns and such—what's the meaning of all this?*

So Jesus launched into a more detailed teaching: "The sower soweth the word" (Mark. 4.14). *Got that part.* The seed we are to sow is the Word of God. *Understood.*

"And these are they by the way side, where the word is sown; but when they have heard, Satan cometh immediately, and taketh away the word that was sown in their hearts" (Mark 4.15).

Jesus seems to be saying, then, that there is some ground (some people) who are of the wayside variety, a soil type in which people are particularly vulnerable to the wiles of satan. He charges right in and almost immediately snatches away the Word we have sown. *A baby disappears.*

"…which are sown on stony ground …immediately receive it with gladness; And have no root in themselves, and so endure but for a time …" (Mark 4.16-17).

What a delight are such exuberant people, those who come to God full of ambition, who whirl and chatter and love everybody in the circle of their widespread arms. Inevitably, though, because they are so shallow, because they have no root and thus no way to take in food, they flounder. They wilt. Their brief dance is finished. *A baby disappears.*

"And these are they which are sown among thorns …and the cares of this world, and the deceitfulness of riches, and the lusts of other things entering in, choke the word, …" (Mark 4.18-19).

Bling. The deadly bling. The baronial house, the sleek boat with hand-rubbed luster, the impressive job, the political clout, and the stock market savvy. Choking lust and life-threatening deceitfulness latch onto the mind of that Christian person— with what rapidity or dawdling moves, who can say?—but as surely as comes the evening sunset, so absolute is the choking of the Word in thorny dirt. *A baby is lost.*

But, Jesus. This is depressing. All this speaking of toxic ground and choking thorns. Is that all there is? Out of this entire planet, must we work only with these kinds of dirt? What of me? Must I be stony or thorny or rootless?

No, of course not. In Mark 4 verse 20, Jesus gets to the better part, the encouraging segment:

"And these are they which are sown on good ground; such as hear the word, and receive it, and bring forth fruit, some thirtyfold, some sixty, and some an hundred."

There is much good ground, fertile and promising. Wide fields will be dug and plowed, and from the amended dirt will the cherished seed sprout. Abundant crops will be harvested before winter, for tender plants will have shot from the warm earth. The scent of flowers will drift on summer breeze. The ground is good.

Now, the lesson for us—a touchy one—and a question. Some people with whom we work are fashioned of undesirable earth. They are stony or thorny, or something about their composition makes them unusually susceptible to satan's snare. They are not good earth. If we expect other than what they are, are we not setting ourselves up for disappointment? This seems to be what Jesus is teaching.

I'm quite taken with my way of writing in which I readily admit to having few answers but many questions. While I think I have something to offer on the subject of backsliding—its cause and prevention—and am setting out a number of pages for you, I am far from thinking I have full comprehension of the matter. So, I am quite comfortable in saying, "I don't know," and "I wonder about this and that."

My question is can we change our earth? If I'm innately stony or thorny, will I bear your digging at me?

The catch is, of course, we don't know which persons are which. I've never seen anyone with a sign hanging about his neck proclaiming, *I'm stony*, or *I'm thorny*, or *take a look at my shallow roots.*

My overriding purpose in discussing this at length is not to determine the deep meaning of each of these soil types but for us to be reminded that such do exist and to be forewarned of the distinct possibility of failure. Some of our converts will backslide, and in some cases, there is little we can do about it. Of course, we will pray and fast and tend and preach and teach. But it seems to be a fact: It is much more difficult to get some people established in the church than it is others. Perhaps it is because of their soil types. Can that be changed? I don't know. I believe it may be possible, but I am not sure. I pray it is.

If we were possessed of unlimited time and energy, this distinction would be less critical, for when we dealt with those of multiple thorns or of a rocky nature, we would not be neglecting that one who is pliable, eager, receptive—the one of good earth.

Pastors struggle with this concept, for their hearts are unique: A shepherd's heart runs to blindness as regards dirt styles. He is passionately tender toward his people, and though in a wrinkle of his mind he may sense a glimmer of the futility of this farming spot, he pleads for time.

Jesus has a story about that very subject:

"...A certain man had a fig tree planted in his vineyard; and he came and sought fruit thereon, and found none. Then said he unto the dresser of his vineyard, Behold, these three years I come seeking fruit on this fig tree, and find none; cut it down; why cumbereth it the ground? And he answering said unto him, Lord, let it alone this year also, till I shall dig about it ..." (Luke 13.6-8).

What then of backsliding and of the lesson Jesus taught of ground? As difficult as it may be to accept, we must recognize that not everyone will stay in the church. Some will backslide, and when we have done all we can to prevent that, while still loving them and praying for them, we must invest our energy in that person of good ground.

The overarching question is how can we be sure? Can we positively identify the ground type? Can such a type be changed? Cannot thorns and stones be removed through love and nurture? Cannot ugly ground be transformed by the Word to workable, pliable soil? The answer is that we must lean on the Holy Ghost and its guidance in this crucial area, doing all we can, but knowing that despite our best efforts, some will backslide. With no haranguing or second-guessing ourselves, we tenderly, and with inevitable sadness, move toward that one of the good earth.

SECTION III
THE RETURN

WORLD'S GREATEST BATTLEFIELD

Neither in war-theatres of Europe, on the blood-soaked earth of America's Civil War, nor in the covert sphere of the elusive terrorist has been fought the world's greatest battle. Nor can one be hand-led to view sacred and hallowed ground as would justify such tag. No. The world's most consequential battlefields are many and are invisible. With no benefit of stone marker, steely monument, or beating flag, the human soul declares for such acclaim.

On this combat zone is effected the ultimate struggle—the battle between God and satan. No days of armistice or suspension of hostilities flare a signal of optimism. Since that staggering day of man's creation, no deferral or truce has been signed, for here in full force is the terminal grappling—the battle for man's soul.

And so has been lodged the premise for a volume to consider the woeful condition of falling away, of sliding back, of spiritual regression—of sin. Now we reach those pages that speak to the certain evasion of such trap and to the glorious restoration of those who have been snared by satan.

Chapter Seventeen
~ Michael's Response ~

After he awoke, Andrew called his brother who was on vacation in Montana and told him of the dream. In the evening, still troubled, Jerry rang Michael's number and told of his own. Silence. Then Mike spoke: "Dad, do you know about Andrew's dream?"

"No."

"Andrew called this morning and told me the same thing. Last night, he too dreamed that I had been killed."

Michael stood riveted to the ground. He had gone from the party to their motor home to get more booze to share when his phone had rung, and his dad had told of the dream. Aghast, he stood beside his motor home. Paralyzed with fear, he thought of the two phone calls: one from his brother, the other now from his father. The details of the dreams differed, but the conclusion was the same—Michael had been killed.

Michael lives with his wife, Melina, in Lake Havasu City, AZ. Life had been good to them in years just past: their construction business was thriving, their children were grown, and they had been blessed with two grandsons, Evin and Gage. In the state of Montana, they had purchased a beautiful recreational vehicle lot, and as often as they could, they drove their rig there for short vacations. They loved Montana so much that later they would find a place to buy. It was a schoolhouse, more than 125 years old, that years before had been converted to a home. A couple had reared their family there, and it would become Mike and Melina's vacation place. Mike keeps an old truck in the barn there, and once, when they could stay more than a few days, they bought baby chicks and yellow ducklings and turned them loose to run around in their yard.

Montana was their dream. Today, as Mike stood beside his motor home, it was a place of nightmare.

"Walk softly before God, Son," his father had said before the conversation ended.

Walk softly before God? How? How could he do that? Michael was a backslider, an acknowledged one, who for more than 25 years had faced away from God and who had thoroughly entangled himself in the world. He worked hard and he played hard. Always the life of the party, his beautiful home with a stunning view of Lake Havasu was frequently the site of exuberant gatherings. He sat often at gaming tables in Las Vegas, and because of the shrewdness of casino managers he was frequently the recipient of complimentary rooms and other plush services. Mike was out of his bailiwick, though, and he never forgot it. He was a prodigal, the son of a loving Father to whom, in essence, Mike had said, "I'll take my inheritance now. I'm leaving home. I'm off to party. I'm off to celebrate." His story was first told in Luke 15.

"And He [Jesus] said, A certain man had two sons: And the younger of them said to his father, Father, give me the portion of goods that falleth to me. And he divided unto them his living. And not many days after the younger son gathered all together, and took his journey into a far country, and there wasted his substance with riotous living. And when he had spent all, there arose a mighty famine in that land; and he began to be in want. And he went and joined himself to a citizen of that country; and he sent him into his fields to feed swine. And he would fain have filled his belly with the husks that the swine did eat: and no man gave unto him. And when he came to himself, he said, How many hired servants of my father's have bread enough and to spare, and I perish with hunger! I will arise and go to my father, and will say unto him, Father, I have sinned against heaven, and before thee, And am no more worthy to be called thy son: make me as one of thy hired servants. And he arose, and came to his father. But when he was yet a great way off, his father saw him, and had compassion, and ran, and fell on his neck, and kissed him. And the son said unto him, Father, I have sinned against heaven, and in thy sight, and am no more worthy to be called thy son. But the father said to his servants, Bring forth the best robe, and put it on him; and put a ring on his hand, and shoes on his feet: And bring hither the fatted calf, and kill it; and let us eat, and be merry: For this my son was dead, and is alive again; he was lost, and is found. And they began to be merry" (Luke 15.11-24).

And so Michael stood bolted to the ground, his face no doubt pale with fear. It was the love of the Father. Had to be. Michael knew that. Two such dreams on the same night were of the hallowed, of the Divine.

There was a shed on the RV property in Montana, and it was there Michael went to weep and to repent. Shuddering, he stood in the presence of God. Trembling, he felt the warm arms of the Father embracing him, and he knew the time had come. The pigpen days were finished. The running was over. Michael had taken his last drink of alcohol.

From a sound sleep, Michael awoke. It was very early the next morning, still dark, and as he roused, he felt his face to be wet, and he heard himself sobbing. Fully awake now, the frightful dreams invaded his mind, causing his heart to pound. He felt a smother of fear. As desperate as a hare in the paw of a timber wolf, so was Michael that morning in Montana. A heavy cloud of conviction engulfed him, pulling him, drawing him. Quietly, so as not to rouse Melina, he slipped from his bed, closed the sliding door, and went to the living room area of the motor home. He sat on the couch.

He began sobbing. *I don't know what to say, God,* he began. *I'm not sure I remember how to pray. I'm sorry, God, I'm sorry.* He mourned and repented and cried, his head a fountain of tears now, his heart ripped apart, his will broken.

When he arrived back home in Lake Havasu, Michael carved out a part of his living room as a sanctuary, a place of repentance and of devotion. Early every morning, he went there for his conversation with God. "I just talked to Him as a friend," Michael has told me more than once. "I didn't say anything fancy. That's not me. I just talked. Just talked as a friend. I confessed all my mistakes, my failures, and my disappointments. I repented again and again." One of the curved ottomans was his altar, and one day, as he knelt there, the Holy Ghost pervaded the room, and Michael began to speak in tongues.

"I tell you that in the same way there will be rejoicing in heaven over one repentant sinner--more rejoicing than over ninety-nine blameless persons who have no need of repentance" (*Weymouth New Testament,* Luke 15.7).

Angels stood by that day in Lake Havasu, perhaps ringing the walls of the Buxton home, where kneeling by a simple piece of furniture was a prodigal, a prodigal come home. The Father was there too, by that ottoman, leaning over His child, that wayward one, that one who had come to himself and who, at last, had come home. Then the Father straightened up and called aloud to one of the servants: *Bring the robe—the best one--and the ring and the new shoes.*

The changing of clothes was invisible. I don't know if it was done in Lake Havasu or in heaven or at a site in between, but I'm sure Michael's ragged clothes and worn out shoes were dumped somewhere, swapped out for heavenly garments, the smell of pig finally gone. *Come here,* Jesus may have said. *Come here, Michael. Turn around now. Let me put this on your shoulders.* And around Michael's trembling body God Himself placed a robe of righteousness.

One more thing: I'm not sure, but I believe I smell a grill firing up!

Chapter Eighteen
The Afterglow of Restoration

Michael's spiritual development was amazing. He was deeply burdened for his colleagues and friends, and after a discussion with his pastor, he began holding Bible studies in his garage with his brother Andrew driving from San Diego to teach the lessons. During those ten months, several were baptized and received the Holy Ghost.

It became increasingly difficult for Andrew to accomplish the ten-hour round trip to teach the Bible studies. After meeting with the United Pentecostal Church, International district board of Arizona, and being sanctioned to officially start a church there, Jerry and I closed up our home in Crestline, loaded our motor home, and went to Lake Havasu to establish a church.

In 1994, Jerry had been severely injured when a drunk driver struck him as Jerry stood by our disabled car. He lay dead in the street. Lorraine Heter had been nearby and had seen him flying through the air. She saw where he landed 86 feet away, rushed over, and revived him. Jerry suffered massive injuries including a broken neck with paralysis, many other broken bones, a damaged heart, damaged kidneys, damaged lungs, and more. His hospital stay was more than four months.[1] Although his recovery was little short of miraculous, Jerry felt it was in the best interest of the church to resign, so in 1996, he retired from being pastor of New Life Center in Rialto, CA (now called Inland Lighthouse Church).

Beyond what we expected following his retirement, Jerry's condition had continued to improve. Both of us were strong and have always had a burden for the work of God. We were available to go to Lake Havasu, willing, and we were very concerned about Michael. So began our stint

---

1 The book, *A Thousand Pieces,* written by Shirley Buxton gives an account of this accident and of the miraculous recovery of Gerald Buxton.

of home missions work. From the first, God blessed us with growth and favor. One of Michael's friends offered the use of a large room in an industrial complex, free of any cost. We gathered chairs, a pulpit, a tiny keyboard, and Michael bought a portable sound system at a local pawnshop. We were in business.

Rev. Rick Faulkner is the regional representative of *Spirit of Freedom Ministries' Christian Intervention Program (CIP)*. Not long after we started the church, which we named Christ Alive Worship Center, Brother Faulkner contacted Jerry about becoming involved in this ministry. Jerry thought about it, prayed about it, and decided to enroll in the program. Michael would be the instructor, Jerry thought.

Later, Michael told us his heart sank when his dad told him about the new program, suspecting that he would be called on to teach it. We were all spread so thin already since there were few of us. In addition, Mike was very busy with his company and with his family obligations.

The program was an instant success in Lake Havasu, far exceeding the expectations of any of us, including, I believe, Rick Faulkner and of those in the *Spirit of Freedom* home office. A burden gripped Michael for those who attended the class, and he began to make a place for the Spirit of God that was definitely moving in the classes. Michael began inviting the students to church. Many of them came, were touched by God, and were filled with the Holy Ghost. When some were ready for baptism, we took them to Mike's pool, where Jerry baptized them in the lovely name of Jesus Christ.

The church grew. The classes grew. The court system had taken notice of the success and appeal of our program, as had the probation department. We had to buy more chairs, and then we needed a larger building. We found a beautiful facility, gulped at the cost, stepped out in faith, and leased it.

Our enrollment reached seventy, necessitating splitting the class, so Michael was now teaching on both Tuesday and Wednesday evenings. He learned to spot those who were hungry for God and often would have intense prayer with them after the regular sessions were finished, sometimes taking them to Jerry's office where he would ask his dad to help them pray. A couple of times, he called me from the front office where I was working on the bookkeeping part of the program to come into the auditorium and to turn on the organ. He passed out church song books, and we sang.

We sang, did Mike and I, as did those CIP students: The students who are in the fight of their lives, the students who are addicts, those who are filled with anger, those who are homeless, those who have no jobs, those who have abandoned their children, those who, themselves, were long ago abandoned.

We sang, did Mike and I, as did those CIP students, the other ones, the other kind: The students who are in the fight of their lives, the students who are addicts, those who are filled with anger but who have good educations and good jobs, or at one time had the good job. They appear successful. They are schoolteachers, restaurant managers, hotel managers, ordained ministers, doctors, and business owners. We sang, did we all, and then it was quiet. For God had moved among us.

The program consists of twenty lessons that are taught on a weekly basis, so there is a steady stream of new people. The face of each new person is scanned for signs of readiness to hear the Gospel.

Michael became the worship leader in the church. I told in earlier pages that sometimes when he was leading songs and felt the need for a drummer, and being the only one available, he would leave the platform, walk to his drums, and lift the worship to another level. Well, at least the worship was lifted to a higher decibel level. Invariably, the CIP students who were there grinned.

In October of 2010, Jerry resigned from being the pastor of Christ Alive Worship Center. He put a new pastor in place, we said our good-byes, gathered our belongings, and from DJ's RV park, Jerry drove our motor home. We headed back to California.

I cried then, as I do now. The crying is of joy because of what God did the short years we were in Lake Havasu: the beautiful building, the excellent reputation we had about town, the peak attendance of 93, the hundreds who had gone through the intervention classes, and the scores who had been baptized and filled with the Holy Ghost.

My joy is for more though, much more. My joy is for Michael, my son. My son, who for more than 25 years had wandered about, a true prodigal. A tender, well-heeled prodigal, he was, but a prodigal nevertheless. A prodigal who had stretches of wallow.

Once Mom, he told me, *I was at a party where they were doing cocaine. You know I drank a lot, but I didn't get involved in drugs very much, but this night I decided to try it. I nearly died. I woke up laid out on a couch, gasping for breath. My chest was moving up and down, but I couldn't get air. I was desperate. I hardly knew what I was doing. I thought I was dying.*

I remember praying. God help me. God please help me. If You will save me, God, I will never do this again. I don't know if I said the words out loud or whether it was just in my head, but I know I meant it. God heard me, and saved me from death. I kept my word; I never touched cocaine again.

Jerry and I agree that without Michael's help, we would not have been able to accomplish what we did during that time in Lake Havasu. Most people visit Christ Alive because of him—either directly or indirectly. (I am uncomfortable making such statements because of Michael being my son, but I don't know another way to do it. In no way do I want to be regarded as bragging about our family, for this is not the case at all. Although I am pinning medals on him today, plenty of times I was sorely ashamed of him.) He is the greatest soul winner I have ever known. Through our many years of pastoring, I cannot recall another lay person who was so passionate about the church, who was so giving, and who was so involved in personal witnessing and soul winning.

Remember. Don't lose sight of that. I am saying these things about a backslider, a backslider of longstanding—one of more than 25 years.

How merciful is our God. How loving He is. How grateful is our family for that long-ago night in August when God's extreme love reached down to the earthly environs of San Diego and of Santa Maria. In the night came the dreams, the dreams that propelled a backslider home.

Chapter Nineteen
～ Jesus Teaches on Restoration ～

G od knows us. God pities us. The Bible says that.

"Like as a father pitieth his children, so the LORD pitieth them that fear him. For he knoweth our frame; he remembereth that we are dust" (Ps. 103.13-14).

Certain portions of Scripture are special to me, and this is one of them. I'm the mother of four children. I love them so much that on occasion when I think about them, in my heart, I feel something akin to literal pain. The vision of their misunderstandings and hurts is of particular grief to me, and I wish it were as easy as when they were small to kiss the tears away or to place a lollipop in each of their fists, and the aches would be gone. One of mine has grave health problems, one was nearly killed in a construction accident, and one has suffered through multiple marital difficulties. Some have struggled financially. Of a sudden, I have seen them stricken: Other times, grim-faced, I watched as they brought calamity down on their own heads. Nothing I could do. Nothing I could say.

I know my children. I know their frame. I pity them.

God knows us. He knows that we are made of dust. He understands and knows our frame. The love and the pity I have for my children is no doubt multiplied many times over within the heart of God. It gives me relief to think of His deep caring for me. I feel a sense of peace as I think of Him watching me as I stumble about, sometimes even to the extent that I lose my footing. He is wise, forgiving, and so understanding. He remembers the day He made me, recalls my physical makeup, my mental capacities, and my emotional order. God has not forgotten that satan is on the loose and that he is out to snare every child of God. He remembers Adam and Eve and that we are forced live in the fallen world in which they blundered. He reckons with the fact that we are still involved in the greatest battle in the world, the battle between good and evil, the fight that takes place within the human soul.

Oh, what a Savior He is. A Savior full of love and compassion, who in that long ago chapter of time, thinking of the inevitability of our falling, arranged a way for us to redeem ourselves. When we are quite unlovable, He loves us. When with sure feet we walk from His presence, He loves us. When satan tricks us, God continues to love us. Despite our foolish moves and our backward stance, God has set up a way for us to redeem ourselves, a place of restoration.

A well-known portion of Scripture in the book of Luke contains the words of Jesus as He taught a lesson on *lostness*: the lost sheep, the lost son, and the lost coin. Pastor Randy Keyes of Modesto, CA has preached a powerful sermon on this subject in which he elucidates the significant differences in these three categories of lost people. I strongly recommend this sermon. (You may contact me to procure a copy of this audiotape.) A couple of chapters back, we spoke extensively about the lost son, the one frequently referred to as the prodigal son. We will consider further that account and take a close look at the other two.

1: THE LOST SHEEP

"And he spake this parable unto them, saying, What man of you, having an hundred sheep, if he lose one of them, doth not leave the ninety and nine in the wilderness, and go after that which is lost, until he find it? And when he hath found it, he layeth it on his shoulders, rejoicing. And when he cometh home, he calleth together his friends and neighbours, saying unto them, Rejoice with me; for I have found my sheep which was lost. I say unto you, that likewise joy shall be in heaven over one sinner that repenteth, more than over ninety and nine just persons, which need no repentance" (Luke 15.3-7).

Lessons for us are numerous in this passage, in which a more beautiful picture of the love of God can hardly be imagined. Each of God's sheep is significant, and although He has many in His flock, when one of us wanders away, He is troubled. He misses us. He loves us, loves us individually, for who we are, for ourselves, alone. Jesus is not comparing us with others. He is not thinking of what we might offer, how beautiful we are, or how talented we may—or may not—be. Those fine, upright ninety-nine who remain—as beautiful as they are, as talented, as faithful—are not enough to satisfy Him. He wants me. He wants you.

Into dependable hands does the Shepherd now place the sheepfold, and into the night air He goes. He's searching, looking, no doubt calling for the lamb who has strayed. He scans the terrain, pushes aside thorns and bushes, and peers down dark crevices. The Shepherd knows how dangerous it is out there, how cold and rocky, and how quickly a lamb might be injured. He knows of the treacherous trails with sharp abutments and sheer cliffs that drop into deep canyons. And so, He searches.

Finally the Shepherd finds the sheep; perhaps it is a lamb, just a baby. It may be bleeding now and no doubt its wooly coat is matted and dirty. It may be injured. For sure, the animal is tired. The Shepherd smiles and bends low to lift the little one, and then He lovingly places His lamb about His neck.

Come over! the Shepherd shouted when he arrived back home where the others waited. Come over, he said to his friends. He knocked on the door of his neighbors and invited them to the party. The lamb is home! The one who was lost, that sweet one who strayed, who did not mean to, but who wandered off, that one who was disillusioned and who was tricked. That one. He's home. Come rejoice with me.

Once again the sheepfold is complete. No one is missing. The lost lamb has been found.

2: THE LOST SON

Pastor Keyes notes the prodigal son's story to differ significantly from that of the lost sheep. The sheep inadvertently wandered away, not really intending to leave the safety of the sheepfold, whereas the prodigal knew exactly what he was doing. Fully aware, he left the father's house. He chose to abandon those riches of the house, deciding instead to become a man of the world. He changed direction, turned away from Father, and headed downward.

In his sermon, Pastor Keyes emphasizes this difference, pointing to the fact that the father did not go after the son as did the Shepherd go after the lost sheep; rather, he let sin work its way in the life of the son. Finally, the lost son slumped to the depth of debauchery and sin. Wallowing in that pigpen, so hungry that he seriously thought of eating the slop that had been thrown to the pigs, he began to think of Father's house. He remembered the glory there, the delicious food. No doubt it was with disgust that he gazed at the rags he was wearing and recalled the fine clothes he used to sport. He began the *coming to himself.* He looked about and saw everything in a different light. The blinders fell from his eyes. No doubt it was with regret that he recalled what he had done, thinking that when he had all that money, he had lots of friends. They had partied, roaring with laughter, but where were they now? Where did they go? Today he was hungry. He was needy. Where were his friends?

This is crazy, the prodigal finally decided. *The servants at Dad's home live better than this. They have good food to eat, nice rooms in which to sleep, and fine clothes to wear.* The prodigal came to himself, and when he did, he no longer looked to the world for help, he no longer looked to his friends, and he knew he certainly couldn't depend on himself. *Look at me. Just look. I'm filthy, broke, homeless, and hungry. And besides that, I'm tending swine, slopping hogs. What am I doing here?*

Instead, he turned his mind toward his father. Filled with guilt concerning his misguided, wasted life, he fixed his gaze toward the father's house. Memories flooded him: The peace that was there, the love, the honesty, the fine music, the banquets, the talks around the fire at night, the parties when friends came over, the aura of honor, the high expectations that filled the atmosphere, the encouragement, the building up, the compliments, and the beauty.

What had he done? How had he made such a tradeoff? How foolish. How disgusting.

He walked off the job, left the sows to squeal through the day and the cornhusks still in their stack. He tromped out of the mud and closed the gate behind him. The prodigal had come to himself. He was heading home.

Once, I heard someone preach that although the father did not go after the son, he had faith that one day he would return, and with that in mind, he kept a calf at the ready. He always had one fattened up so that on the day of the return, all would be in order for the celebration. Father didn't know it yet, but today was the day. Down the road came a man. He was not riding in a cart or on an animal; he was walking. A slow figure, bent. As the father looked, he saw there was something familiar about the figure: the way he walked, the way he held his head, that slight kick of the heel as he took each step. It reminded him of someone. That wasn't a stranger. That was someone he knew.

Father moved further from the house and closer to the road, shielding his eyes with his hands so he could see better. The traveler lifted his head, and now the father knew. That was his son! From a long way off, he began to run down the road, his fine robes billowing behind him, and then they were together. The father embraced his son and fell on his neck, filled with compassion.

"I have sinned against heaven, and in thy sight, and am no more worthy to be called thy son," the prodigal repented (Luke 15.21).

Having compassion on his boy, understanding his frame and how he was made, the father ignored the words of the prodigal. *Bring the robe,* the father called to a servant. *The best one. Bring new shoes and a ring for his finger. My son has come home!*

Perhaps it was another servant the father drew aside. Perhaps he whispered in his ear, *The calf. That special one. The one we have been fattening up these long days. Kill it. Start the fires, prepare the banquet. Let us make merry. My son was lost, but is found. He was dead, but is alive!*

3: THE LOST COIN

The third parable Jesus tells in his discourse of the lost has to do with an inanimate object, a coin:

"Or suppose a woman has ten silver coins and loses one. Does she not light a lamp, sweep the house and search carefully until she finds it? And when she finds it, she calls her friends and neighbors together and says, 'Rejoice with me; I have found my lost coin.' In the same way, I tell you, there is rejoicing in the presence of the angels of God over one sinner who repents" (*NIV*, Luke 15.8-10).

These parables make it clear that Jesus was acutely aware of the inherent danger of backsliding among His people. His long reach and magnificent teaching are extended to every Christian, for think about it: Jesus must be warning Christians, as by definition, it is only a Christian who can backslide. The inference from these teachings is compelling: We need to listen—all of us. May our hearing be sensitive—bell-like in its clarity. For none is exempt from the danger of slipping away. No one. Yes, we are to have confidence in God and in His Spirit that leads us, but without exception, we must be watchful, ever vigilant, always aware of the deviousness of satan. He may blindside us. He probably will work right inside the church itself, using multiple ploys and stratagems. Paul warns of this danger:

"So, if you think you are standing firm, be careful that you don't fall" (*NIV*, 1 Cor. 10.12).

This last parable in the series speaks of a person who is lost in the house. It seems sound interpretation of the passage to suggest that the house may well refer to the Church. In his timely sermon, Pastor Keyes takes us one step further, pointing to a preacher as being the one who sweeps and cleans, carefully searching for the lost coin, the lost person.

Being an inanimate object, a coin, differing from the lost sheep and the lost son, does not know it is lost. An alarming thought is that we could be part of a church, sitting in our favored place, faithfully attending the services, and be lost. I don't want to be lost in the house of God. I want the man of God to sweep vigorously as he searches for me. Don't spare me, Pastor. Don't spare me, Evangelist. Be prayerful and thoughtful as you bend the broom and as the dust flies, but don't stop your search for me. Don't grow weary because you can't find me. Don't store your broom in the closet of indifference or discouragement. Don't leave me in a dark corner, for remember, I cannot find myself. How can I? I don't even know I'm lost.

I mentioned it in an earlier part of this book, but I want to emphasize again how powerful is the preaching of God's Word. It truly is of another world, transforming mere men into the voice of God. I've seen it happen multiplied times over, and it never fails to produce a sense of wonder in me. It is amazing. So then, when I come into the church, looking the part, smiling left and right, and sitting properly on my pew, remember, I may be lost. Pastor, please light the lamp. Assure that the chamber is filled with oil and that the wick is turned high. Turn the light in every direction, refusing to fear dark corners. That difficult angle, the hard one to reach? Poke in there with your broom, for it may be there I will be found. For if I am a lost coin, I am as lost as the totally unregenerate. I am a sinner, away from God.

Dr. Richard C. Trench is among those scholars who compare the woman in this parable to the Church. His book *Trench on the Parables* is a magnificent work. (Long out of print, my treasured copy bears the signature of the first owner of the volume and the hand-written date of 1875. Copies of the text may be obtained on the Internet.)

The other two parables focus on the condition of the lost person, but this one, says Dr. Trench, deals more with the sorrow of the one who has lost the coin. She has contributed to the loss, says Dr. Trench, for while a sheep may stray of itself, *"a piece of money could only be missing by a certain negligence on the part of such as should have kept it."*

There is truth here. Facing truth often rankles the soul, perturbing us and causing certain uneasiness. Oh, facing truth comes painlessly if we're standing on the favored side of the line, but let the glow of truthful clarity shine harshly on our own faces, and it is likely we may shrink from such illumination. I have vigorously seen to the integrity of this book, and toward the conclusion here, I must do no less. Lest I be thought judgmental or lest I should I overstep my bounds, especially when addressing those in ministry, I have been vastly careful as I have voiced my concerns. More than one time during this writing, I spent hours on the construction of only one paragraph or of only a few lines, needing to say the words but sincerely wanting to avoid offense.

Dr. Trench may be right. *There must have been negligence.* And it is quite possible that I participated in such negligence. I was inattentive. I was unmindful. For do I not have the Holy Ghost? Am I not part of the church? I know I am light, for Jesus said it:

"Ye are the light of the world. A city that is set on an hill cannot be hid. Neither do men light a candle, and put it under a bushel, but on a candlestick; and it giveth light unto all that are in the house" (Matt. 5.14-15).

Do I not have the Word of life?

"...among whom ye shine as lights in the world; Holding forth the word of life (Phil. 2.15-16).

I am not the pastor, nor is it my place to take corrective action if I see the threat of dark corners or even full-blown signs of backsliding. But I am part of the church, and it is my obligation to spread light, to push aside darkness, and to talk about the Word of God.

An interesting Scripture is found in Ephesians 5.13:

"But all things that are reproved are made manifest by the light: for whatsoever doth make manifest is light."

Without overstepping my bounds as a saint of God, it should be that this light of the Holy Ghost I possess will prickle the one who sits beside me, that one who may have started a gentle slide back. If I'm concerned about a brother or a sister, and ask God to guide me as I try to help them, surely the light of God will reveal those hidden, questionable areas.

And to the ministry, I plead again that you reprove us. "For the things that are reproved are made manifest." Now we can see them. We see the error in our ways. Suddenly, we know we have fallen; we have become dusty. We were lost there for a little while, but through the illumination of the Word of God, through some vigorous sweeping, we are found.

Accounts of medical malpractice never fail to shock us. We are appalled when we hear of a strong limb being amputated instead of the infected one or a healthy eye being removed instead of the blind one. When we are sick or injured, we go to the doctor or the hospital with an expectation of at least improvement, if not of complete cure. No wonder that when such medical errors occur, we are frightened and angry. It startled me a few days ago to read that medical error is the third-largest cause of death in the United States.

"According to Dr. Barbara Starfield of the Johns Hopkins School of Hygiene and Public Health, 250,000 deaths per year are caused by medical errors, making this the third-largest cause of death in the US, following heart disease and cancer." (www.jhsph.edu)

While none would argue against the worth of a healthy body, and while any rational person would be distressed at such an account of deaths caused by medical error, all Christians will agree that the soul is of infinitely more value than the body. Ghastly, then, to consider is that our treatment of persons who sit beside us or in front of us in our churches might be damaged—perhaps terminally—by our actions or lack of action. God help us. God help me.

More than one common thread runs through Jesus' teachings on these three parables. One of the most significant is that once the lost were found, there was great rejoicing. Whether it was the return of the sheep, the son, or the coin, a celebration was called, a party was thrown, and a fat calf was roasted. The angels of heaven joined those who on the earth celebrated. So did Jesus. I see Him laughing and hugging and rejoicing. His child was safely home. Party time in heaven!

Chapter Twenty
Restoration Ponderings

erhaps as should be, the greater part of this book on backsliding has dealt with ways to avoid the condition. Would that none of us strayed, that none were deceived, that none had chanced to lose that first love. A sterling section in the history of backsliders would be that of a blank page, a withholding of the pen, and a final closing of the book. Oh, that none of us would ever turn away from Jesus and head again into the world. Well-spent, then, are the numerous pages that speak to the prevention of falling away.

Precision of saying and soul-honesty urge me to concede, however, of the high likelihood of a passing lapse in the godly design of all of us. But for a moment, perhaps, yet was it done; our feet slipped. Not much. Just a little. Quickly, we pulled back and righted ourselves. In all probability, no one was aware, for hardly had we known ourselves. Perhaps it was a sermon that caught us, or a passage of Scripture we read in our morning time with God, or maybe it was just a nudge. A God-nudge. So in the literal sense, if all would be revealed, it is predictable that every Christian would be shown to have at one moment or another, and to some slight degree, slipped back. Helps with compassion, doesn't it? Keeping the stones of condemnation clenched within our fists is much easier if we are figures of truth who keep in focus our own missteps.

Yet, in the fullest sense when we speak of backsliding, we have referred to those who somehow were not able to stop the backward spin. They justly were termed *backsliders*, and with good reason we have contemplated their fall in the hope that we could avoid such a happening.

We have arrived now at the extremely important spot in this book where we speak of restoration and of its different facets. It will help us if we view it from several angles, including that of what the backslider himself should do.

1: REPENTANCE OF THE BACKSLIDER

What it takes to jolt the backslider into returning home is numerous and varied. In the prodigal son's case, it was hunger; it was that he had reached the bottom and that he was sick of it. It was the memory of his home. In Michael's case, it was phone calls telling the dreams of his death. For some, it is an internal urging, a tugging of the Holy Ghost. A dear friend of mine said his losing his job, his security, and his friends precipitated his return. He had sunk to the bottom, and he felt helpless. *"It was the only time I have ever asked for help,"* he told me. Others have come into a church service, and the preaching has pricked their hearts, and when the call is given, they walk to that hallowed place. It may be the death of a loved one, a severe automobile accident, or a life-threatening illness that is the catalyst that causes the prodigal to say, *"I've had enough of this. I want to go home."*

However, we are summoned, regardless of the method by which we arrive, when we sink into place at God's altar, it is surely with great weeping and with urgent repentance. For are not our hearts broken? Are we not guilty? Have we not fallen into the dregs? Have we not shamed God and His church? And so we repent. We cry, and with great groaning, we wrestle with ourselves and with our evil ways. We may have no words, only fountains of tears and moans of grief. We repent. We submit.

We would do well to take the words of Jeremiah as our own:

"Heal me, O LORD, and I shall be healed; save me, and I shall be saved: for thou art my praise" (Jer. 17.14).

What a prayer from this great prophet, a prayer that should flow easily and often from our lips. In our altars of repentance, we are opening our hearts, hiding nothing from God. Tears gush as we show Him our wounds. *These need healed, God. I'm pretty beaten up from my stint out there in the world. Lots of injuries, lots of hurt. I need your healing, God. I'm suffering. Save me. Heal me.*

Jeremiah writes also in 14.7:

"O LORD, though our iniquities testify against us, do thou it for thy name's sake: for our backslidings are many; we have sinned against thee."

Interestingly, even though God knows everything about us, even to the number of hairs on our heads (Luke 12.7), He wants us to confess our needs. Some people have difficulty doing this, but it is important that we press beyond any hindrance that would keep us from full repentance. God wants to hear our voices. David had learned that lesson, and in Psalm 142 prays a magnificent prayer:

"I cried unto the LORD with my voice; with my voice unto the LORD did I make my supplication. I poured out my complaint before him; I shewed before him my trouble. When my spirit was overwhelmed within me, then thou knewest my path. In the way wherein I walked have they privily laid a snare for me. I looked on my right hand, and beheld, but there was no man that would know me: refuge failed me; no man cared for my soul. I cried unto thee, O LORD: I said, Thou art my refuge and my portion in the land of the living. Attend unto my cry; for I am brought very low: deliver me from my persecutors; for they are stronger than I. Bring my soul out of prison, that I may praise thy name: the righteous shall compass me about; for thou shalt deal bountifully with me."

And to you who have returned home and kneel now at God's altar, but whose head is so heavy and whose embarrassment and burden of guilt are great, I refer you again to a Psalm:

"But thou, O LORD, art a shield for me; my glory, and the lifter up of mine head" (3.3).

It is not only you, my friend who reads here today, who have been low. Each of us has been so confused, so disappointed in others and in ourselves, so troubled by challenges of life that we have slumped in despair. We have been depressed, and we have been embarrassed.

On a common plane, our heads have hung low, too weary to lift, too empty to cry another tear. Then Jesus came by. Bending low, He tenderly slipped an arm under our fallen shoulders and with His own loving hands He lifted our heads.

2: God receives us

These items are taken from the journal of a backslider who was working his way back into God's fold.

Am I ready for the change?
Am I serious?
Do I mean business?
Will I make it this time?
God, I am miserable! I want you, not religion!

Church was good today. Moving closer to a decision. Love all I hear. But I am afraid. I do not want to fail God, again.
At altar calls I normally slip out or kneel silently where I am. Tonight I knelt and prayed for forgiveness. I have made lots of errors and failures. I know God can but will he forgive ALL I have done? I am going to keep on seeking.

I suspect that every backslider who has considered returning to God has met with the thought of God not wanting him back. Have I gone too far? Have I stepped over the line? His mind is filled with memories of his wretched, ungodly life, and he has full understanding of just what he has done. He has trampled the blood of Calvary beneath his feet.

But listen to the words of God as He speaks of the backslider:

"I will heal their backsliding, I will love them freely: for mine anger is turned away from him" (Hos. 14.4).

Oh, what a Savior. What love, what forgiveness.

"For I know the thoughts that I think toward you, saith the LORD, thoughts of peace, and not of evil, to give you an expected end. Then shall ye call upon me, and ye shall go and pray unto me, and I will hearken unto you. And ye shall seek me, and find me, when ye shall search for me with all your heart. And I will be found of you, saith the LORD: and I will turn away your captivity ..." (Jer. 29.11-14).

"I cried unto the LORD with my voice, and he heard me out of his holy hill. Selah" (Ps. 3.4).

None of your concerns, dear backslider, pose any difficulty for God; none of the complications, fears, or apprehension challenges Him in the least. When you cried out, He heard you, He forgave you, His anger dissolved. For it was out of His holiness that He listened and from His righteous nature that He made the promise: *Seek me and you will find me. I don't think evil of you, Child. I think peace. I think heaven. You are forgiven.*

3: The church's part in restoration

"One of the most infamous incidents in New York City history was the 1964 stabbing death of a young Queens woman by the name of Kitty Genovese. Genovese was chased by her assailant and attacked three times in the street. Over the course of half an hour, 38 of her neighbors watched from their windows. During that time, however, none of the 38 witnesses called the police." *(27).* —Malcolm Gladwell *The Tipping Point*

A brother has fallen; a gap has developed within the church. A pew is empty. Because we truly care and because we love this person, we will do all we can to bring about restoration. We may be uncertain how to proceed, surely not wanting to cause offense or to contribute to the further decline of our brother. Yet, in our spirits, we have a sense of burden and of loss. We pray and ask God to direct us, to give us His mind, His understanding, to flood our thoughts with wisdom. We have no feeling of superiority or of judgment, but of compassion and fear for their eternal destination.

While we struggle with knowing the best way to proceed, we love our fallen brother, and we have determined we will fight for him. Precedent extends to Nehemiah 4.14:

> "And I looked, and rose up, and said unto the nobles, and to the rulers, and to the rest of the people, Be not ye afraid of them: remember the Lord, which is great and terrible, and fight for your brethren, your sons, and your daughters, your wives, and your houses."

When he was a teenager, for a significant period of time our youngest son, Andrew, struggled in his walk with God. He wanted to do right, and even at that early age knew the ministerial call of God was on his life. But he was floundering. Of course, Jerry and I were troubled deeply about this. To the end of my life, I will be grateful to Pastor Jim Shoemake and his wife, Bobby, who played such a big part in saving Andrew. He moved to San Jose and began attending their church. They nurtured him. They fought for him. Within a short time, Pastor Shoemake called Jerry to tell him how well Andrew was doing and what a blessing he had become to the church.

And so we fight. We fight all. We fight for our brothers, for those who are struggling and who are gasping for spiritual breath. We rally about them, and come the day when one walks out the door of the church, we continue our wrestling and our engaging in prayer for them.

This period of backsliding may be short, but sadly, in many cases, it is of long duration, often of a great number of years. We persist in caring, in praying, in asking for direction from God. We will not shun the backslider, although it is a mistake to compromise our own journey toward godliness and righteousness by participating in the sinful ways in which he now indulges. Such action is a dreadful mistake, and while at the moment he may seem pleased should we do so, in his deep heart, he will be disappointed at our failure to stand for our own principles.

I have a friend who was a backslider for more than 30 years, but who has recently come back to God. I asked him to share his thoughts about what we in the church can do to help bring about restoration. He answered in this way: *"Let those outside know that we care and prayers are being made. Remain honest and approachable and know all the signs of hunger that come from inside."*

Paul addressed the subject in Galatians 6.1:

"Brethren, if a man be overtaken in a fault, ye which are spiritual, restore such an one in the spirit of meekness; considering thyself, lest thou also be tempted."

If ever the love of God needs to be working in our lives, it is during these times when we try to help someone find his way back to God. With humility and great care, we minister to this loved one. We consider his personality, his emotional state, and his spiritual awareness. We heed Paul's injunction: We consider ourselves, think of our own weaknesses, and remember the times when we too, most likely, had taken a little step backward.

Our ways are gentle. We are dealing with a person who has been desperately wounded, who is bleeding and broken. When an ambulance arrives at a hospital with a person just wrenched from a mutilated automobile, the doctors and nurses don't jerk him around, nor sling him carelessly onto an operating table. They treat him with care, staunch the blood flow, bind up the broken parts, and prescribe for his pain. The backslider in our altar is every bit as desperately in need of tender care as is the patient at our local hospital. His brokenness must be seen to, his pain acknowledged, his bleeding staunched.

"Let your gentleness be evident to all. The Lord is near" (*NIV*, Phil. 4.5).
"By the meekness and gentleness of Christ, I appeal to you" (*NIV*, 2 Cor. 10.1).

We who are the strong ones and who are helping the backslider as he makes his way home should avoid any semblance of the attitude of the elder son (Luke 15.25-32), who became angry because of the celebration over the return of his brother. Never should such a loathsome attitude have play in any of our churches. Rather than being jealous over his being restored to a previous place of honor, we should help the prodigal attain that place. The unique gifts and abilities our brother once possessed are still there. The call of God that once was on his life still remains: "God's gifts and his call are irrevocable" (*NIV*, Rom. 11.29).

Neither confusion nor shock should come about when that one who fell away is restored to a high place, for before his birth, he was ordained by purpose of God.

> "Who hath saved us, and called us with an holy calling, not according to our works, but according to his own purpose and grace, which was given us in Christ Jesus before the world began " (2 Tim. 1.9).

Inescapable, though, is that the restored backslider will pay a heavy toll for his misdeeds. The noblest plan God had for his life is likely relegated to that of the lesser.

4: HEAVY PRICE PAID BY THE BACKSLIDER

A necessary part of this work is the consideration of the price the backslider must pay for that period of time in which he strayed, that unforgettable interval when he was living a life of rebellion and of sinfulness. While God has shown His boundless mercy, and full restoration has taken place, it cannot be denied that sin will exact its payment. My friend says, *"I have paid the highest price imaginable for what I have done. "*

One of Michael's deep regrets is that he failed to train his children in the ways of the Lord. "I was partying, Mom," he has said more than once. "I didn't take them to church. I didn't teach them how to live right."

A person who falls away from God and who during his time away marries outside the faith has set himself up for significant hurt. For once he returns to God, his worldview will totally change, and unless his spouse chooses the same life, there will be conflict. No matter how loving the couple, nor how diligently they strive for cohesiveness in their home, the discord will be great. Incompatibility between the principles and interests of the couple would be hard to deny.

Consider this aspect: the unsaved spouse, through no personal fault, has had his life upset in many ways. Some of the places the couple used to go and some of the activities with which they were previously involved are not conducive to that of a dedicated Christian. So, although he may in good conscience attend these places alone, no longer will they as a couple be so involved. His life has been disrupted.

Such a marriage can endure, though; indeed, in many ways, it will grow stronger, for now God has become a powerful force within the walls of this home. His favor is there. The spouse who has returned to God will demonstrate a sweeter attitude, will be kinder and more loving than before. He will manifest the traits of God.

"Wives, in the same way be submissive to your husbands so that, if any of them do not believe the word, they may be won over without words by the behavior of their wives."

This is Peter's writing in 1 Peter 3.1 (*NIV*), and though it clearly is addressed to women, it seems appropriate to think the husband of an unbelieving wife may entertain the same promise. You may well win your spouse to God by your holy and righteous ways.

Wisdom in its highest form is urged in these cases. I've been impressed by the thoughtfulness of restored brothers who sensibly set the tenor of godliness in their divided homes. They sincerely respect the rights and ideals of their spouses. They love them for their good qualities and acknowledge their beautiful ways.

Yet, loneliness will be a significant part of that person's life, for it may be that by himself, he attends church and engages in its varied functions. One of the most painful aspects is the difficulty of talking of the spirit of God with his spouse. Understanding is just not there, and when such conversations arise, a blank look is observed, an emptiness of comprehension. Of anointed preaching where the Word of God becomes a fiery flame, of soaring majestic worship where the soul is lifted in ecstasy, of altars filled with the hungry—of these and others there can be no spiritual handling, there can be no talk of the heart.

Another price paid by backsliders is that of awful memories, of recalling days and nights so filled with raucous abandonment that the thoughts bring only shame. Certainly, not every amusement and entertainment with which a backslider involves himself is sinful. But it is empty when you have laid God aside, and instead you have filled your life with the pleasures of the world. "It cannot be denied, Mom," Michael has said to me often. "There are fun and pleasure in the world, and not all of it is sinful or damaging to one's soul. But it is empty, so lacking in substance and real meaning." He has told me of lying on his bed at night after a party thinking of God and feeling alone and desolate. He reminisced about God's people, his longtime friends, about church services, about the sweet presence of God. Sometimes he cried.

It may be that once a person flagrantly backslides, he has opened himself to a full attack of satan and that the use of alcohol and other mind-altering drugs may allow an evil holding on that person's mind. Deplorable memories of such satanic advancement often remain with a restored person. It was not long after Michael's return to God that the devil first invaded his bedroom. From a sound sleep, he awoke in terror, petrified, soaked in a puddle of sweat. It seemed as though someone were in the room: He sensed an evil presence. Voiceless with dread, he could not cry out. He learned to keep a Bible on his nightstand, and when these spirits come against him, he reaches for his Bible and places it on his chest. It has been years since this first occurred, and although it is with less frequency now, satan continues his attack on Michael through his mind and through foul memories.

My friend says, *"What is most painful and it haunts me daily, is what I have failed to do for God. I continue to question whether I can ever forget what I have failed to do."* I know this gentleman well. He is talented, kind, and intelligent, one that God had selected to carry the Gospel. No wonder he speaks of being haunted by the thought of his 31 years of rejecting God's plan for his life. While I do not in any way want to contribute to his grief, nor to castigate him, it is honest, and it is to the point of this book to consider what could have been had he chosen otherwise.

Michael, also, lives with such thoughts, as surely must the multitude of other prodigals who have returned home. Yesterday, as we spoke on the phone about this subject, Michael said, "Mom, I can think of more than one person who I ran with during those years, and to whom I did not witness—who are now dead."

It is not easy for a backslider to point to the cross of Calvary.

Chapter Twenty-One
Of Cankerworm and Caterpillar

I begin this final chapter by noting that in Michael's possession today is an important set of papers—papers that once filled out and then approved by a council will induct him into a body of preachers. He is to become a licensed minister of the Gospel of Jesus Christ.

"And the floors shall be full of wheat, and the fats shall overflow with wine and oil. And I will restore to you the years that the locust hath eaten, the cankerworm, and the caterpiller, and the palmerworm, my great army which I sent among you.

And ye shall eat in plenty, and be satisfied, and praise the name of the LORD your God, that hath dealt wondrously with you: and my people shall never be ashamed. And ye shall know that I am in the midst of Israel, and that I am the LORD your God, and none else: and my people shall never be ashamed.

And it shall come to pass afterward, that I will pour out my spirit upon all flesh; and your sons and your daughters shall prophesy, your old men shall dream dreams, your young men shall see visions: And also upon the servants and upon the handmaids in those days will I pour out my spirit" (Joel 2.24-29).

During the years Michael was away from God, it never occurred to me as I prayed for his return that he would one day be a preacher. My mind never conjured up such a thought. I just wanted him saved. I wanted him back in the church. I wanted him home with God. I lift high this example of the compassion of God for no personal advantage, but that you may further know the wondrous mercy and love of our incredible God. I spotlight its telling to give you faith and the determination to stay your own feet from backsliding. The account is for you who have a loved one who is lost, for you who cry in the night for your son or your daughter, and finally for you who yourself have fallen away and are tonight a backslider.

No, I had no thought of Michael becoming a preacher. I had no vision of him teaching hundreds of people in Lake Havasu, nor of him teaching Sunday morning adult classes or Wednesday night Bible studies. I just wanted him saved. I wanted him to rap on his drums again. I wanted him to dance in the spirit once more.

But his ground was desolate, for locusts and caterpillars had eaten away at his pastures; he was bare as a frozen wilderness. Evil armies had plundered his house. His losses were appalling. Great was his defeat. Heavy had been his fall.

Then, one August day, he came to himself. Rousing from his degenerate state, he wept bitter tears of sore repentance. And so began the restoration. The oil and wine of the Holy Ghost commenced their abundant flow and lush fruit appeared on the trees. Within the barn, the stalls were stuffed to fullness and the stacks of wheat towered high. Cool water gushed over the land.

That eaten by the locust was replaced. That chewed up by the caterpillar was rejuvenated. That gnawed on by the palmerworm was restored. *Abundance* was a word often heard. Banquet tables were spread in sumptuous form; the harvest was rich. The years lost were somehow regained. Amazing. Only by the amazing grace of God can be seen such restoration.

In the concluding pages of this book, I am directing a few words smack into the hideous, despicable face of beelzebub, that great dragon, the old slew foot. I speak this injunction forcefully and authoritatively, for they are God's words spoken through His prophet, Micah, in chapter 7, verse 8. Not only for me, but for all who read here, I vigorously utter this commandment:

"Rejoice not against me, O mine enemy:

when I fall, I shall arise[!]"

Afterword
The Altar Call

I've never given an altar call before, and I suspect that I may never give another one, but I'm calling one this evening. It will be short. I'm alone here in the house as I finish this work, and my burden for its telling is as intense as it was that long ago moment when I made the first markings that would develop into this book. This is the fourth book I have written. I have put my best effort into the writing and publishing of them, and I am pleased with their content and with their appearance. I think I did the best I could on each of them. But for none did I have the passion I have for this one.

Likely, Michael's straying from God and then returning plays a major role in the burden I feel for these pages, although I have come to think there may be more at work than that. Throughout my lifetime, my close association with churches has given me the opportunity to observe, in a fairly intimate way, many people who are Christians and who make up local church bodies. I've known their struggles, their successes, and their failures. I've seen them hurt, and I've seen them abundantly happy. I've seen too many of them—good people—leave the church.

And so, the altar call.

If you've forgotten, please turn to the introduction of the book where I state that this book is not one of judgment. I have not tried to convince others that they are backsliders, and in no way have I endeavored to erect a framework in which I wish to scrutinize lines and boundaries over which some may have crossed. This is a straightforward book on ways to avoid backsliding and on helping restore those who have done so. With all humbleness and with keen awareness of my own multiple flaws, I say these things. I strive to keep my heart with all diligence. I repent daily and only have full assurance of my salvation when I stand at the foot of the cross.

This altar call is for backsliders. Multitudes are out there: you are fine people who have strayed and who are too good to miss heaven. I'm asking you to return home. It is not God's will that you continue with your back toward Him. Bear with me as I ask how we can think to stand against God? We are but insects, a flicker in the night of the universe, a speck.

> "But who are you, O man, to talk back to God? Shall what is formed say to him who formed it, 'Why did you make me like this?'" (*NIV*, Rom. 9.20).

Yet, because of hurts and misunderstandings, we oppose God: We have separated ourselves from His people. We who were once of His throne room, we who once carried His holy scent on our hands, have turned to another. I'm giving an altar call.

I cannot do much. I am not positioned for greatness or for wide effectiveness, but I can do this. I'm praying that God will use this simple book to speak to backsliders wherever you are. You know what to do. You know where to go. May a veritable torrent become a gushing river that will sweep through our land, taking back to our altars those who have wandered, but who, at the last, are finished with straying and who have decided to return home. With love and forgiveness in His eyes, God is waiting, and so are we.

About Shirley Buxton

Gerald and Shirley Buxton

Shirley celebrates life. Full of zest and energy, she continues to take interest in a wide sweep of the world. She is an avid amateur photographer, adventurous, and ready to travel at the mention of the word.

Her deepest joy comes from her close relationship with Jesus and from her family. She and Gerald have been married fifty-five years, and are supremely blessed in that all four of their children are serving God. Her three sons are ministers of the Gospel, as is one of her grandsons.

Since childhood, she has been ardently involved in the work of God, and has been a minister's wife most of her adult years. Several years after his retirement from New Life Center in Rialto, CA, Gerald and Shirley went to Lake Havasu City, AZ, where for three and a half years, they worked to plant a church. The venture was successful; scores of people have been baptized and have been filled with the Holy Ghost. During those years, a church was solidly built, and an exceptionally successful Christian Intervention program was established. It continues to flourish.

Shirley speaks a few times throughout the year at local churches, seminars and ladies conferences. Writing is one of her passions. She writes daily; has contributed to various publications and has authored three other books.

MORE BOOKS
BY SHIRLEY BUXTON

A THOUSAND PIECES (4th printing)
"A Thousand Pieces is a powerful, emotional, faith-building account of one man's struggle for life."
—*Rev. Berl Stevenson*

ROAD TALES
"The Buxtons are exciting people, and it has been a joy to know them. Their experiences and travels have often put us on our knees, but victory is a word they frequently use, because God does deliver them."
—*Rev. Paul Price*

LINK TO EXCELLENCE
"Link to Excellence is a thought-provoking book that will cause women to seek to do things right, and is a great addition to every woman's library."
—*Joy Haney*

You may contact her at shirleybuxton@gmail.com for more information about any of these books.

BLOGS BY SHIRLEY BUXTON

writenow.wordpress.com
shirleybuxton.wordpress.com
shirleybuxtonphotography.wordpress.com

What People Are Saying

"BACKSLIDING...the bitter bite of beelzebub, is an intriguing study of a real and present danger for all Christians. There are outstanding insights for pastors as well as for church members. This kind of wisdom is born only out of ministering to thousands of people.... Exceptionally written,...it closes with a message of mercy, hope and faith."

—Rev. David Elms, pastor, writer

"This book kept me up late into the night thinking of so many faces that I have seen walk away from the church. Shirley Buxton has stirred my spirit again with her pen. ...I intend on keeping this book easily accessible, not only as a reference tool, but as a source of inspiration and faith that the "backslider" can come home. Thank you Shirley Buxton for a job well done!"

—Rev. Myles Young, pastor, recording artist

"BACKSLIDING: the bitter bite of beelzebub" is rock solid to the core and reflects the care, compassion and the character of a wise First Lady of the Gospel. The message of this manuscript needs to be downloaded into the hearts of Christian pastors and practitioners alike."

—Rev. Howard Pastorella, Director, Spirit of Freedom Ministries

"Just finished reading your new book manuscript on backsliding. I read it in three sittings. I was driven to tears, joy and excitement....This should be a church resource...Excellent."

—Rev. Leon Frost, pastor

Shirley Buxton has addressed an urgent need facing the church: and she has done it with the compassionate heart of a mother. Challenges face every generation and this (backsliding) is one of our greatest.

—Rev. Gary Hogan, pastor, superintendent Arizona District UPCI